CREATING YOUR

FOREVER
FAMILY

For my family

How to Incorporate
Family Proclamation Principles into Your Home

CREATING YOUR

FOREVER FAMILY

Rachel A. Sullivan

Covenant Communications, Inc.

Cover images: *Family Icon* © MicrovOne, iStockphotography.com. *Salt Lake Temple* © Covenant Communications.

Cover design by Christina Marcano © 2018 by Covenant Communications, Inc.

Published by Covenant Communications, Inc.
American Fork, Utah

Printed in the United States of America
First Printing: September 2018

24 23 22 21 20 19 18   10 9 8 7 6 5 4 3 2 1

ISBN: 978-1-52440-677-6

ACKNOWLEDGMENTS

Years ago a personal need for parenting help started me on a research project that eventually became this book. Along the way I was bolstered by loving, supportive, and encouraging family and friends. I never would have begun writing without the persistent encouragement of my wonderful husband, Cameron. Thank you for believing in me and being so helpful throughout the entire process—scanning and copying sources and being my computer guru, as well as cooking, running errands, and caring for our small, energetic tribe time after time while I researched, wrote, and revised. Thanks also to each of our children—Jacob, Abigail, Grace, and Emma—who were patient and understanding when Mom was tied up with the computer again and again. I am blessed to be your mother.

Many friends and loved ones shared encouragement, ideas, tips, and successes or reviewed early versions of my manuscript. Thanks to Mindy McQuivey, Camille Warnick, Paul and Betsy Werrett, Deanna Leonard, Tiffany Bowen, Sharalyn Slaugh, Rachel Sargent, Auralie Jones, Bryce and Aubree Shelley, Kristen Gipson, Barbara Higgins, Cathy Croxton, Christine Sullivan, and Kellene Adams for your individual wisdom, goodness, and experience.

Thanks to Kami Hancock at Covenant Communications for her insightful edits and for patiently and cheerfully guiding me through the publishing process. Thanks also to Christina Marcano and the graphic design team for designing the cover and to Stephanie Lacy for her marketing expertise.

Finally, and most importantly, I am indebted to my Father in Heaven, who gently led and inspired me in a process of research, writing, and application that has shaped me as a person. I will be forever grateful for the journey.

TABLE OF CONTENTS

INTRODUCTION

The home is the laboratory of our lives, and what we learn there largely determines what we do when we leave there. —Thomas S. Monson[1]

PARENTHOOD PRESENTS SOME OF LIFE'S deepest joys and greatest struggles. From the moment your first child is placed in your arms, you are forever changed. You have accepted a heavenly calling with no release. You have been given an opportunity to become like God, to come to know Him better as you strive to help Him parent His children. It is a daunting task for even the most spiritually capable.

A gospel perspective makes parenthood simpler and more far-reaching. We realize our children are first children of our Father in Heaven. He cares about them, and He is actively involved in raising them; we are invited to learn from Him in the process. We know where to turn with our questions and heartaches. At the same time, we must realize that while we raise our families, we are not simply raising our children. We are raising the leaders of the next generation. We are raising the parents of our grandchildren. We must focus on raising a generation that is firmly grounded and converted to Christ and can stand strong in the face of tremendous challenges. The world we raise our children in is darker and wickeder than the world in which we grew up. The world our grandchildren will live in will be darker still. We must raise children who can stand strong and faithful in the days to come.

The best way to prepare our children to spiritually thrive in today's world and in the future is to build homes that are filled with light—the light that comes solely from pure gospel living. We must soak up that light through our personal spirituality. We cannot be casual in our discipleship and our efforts to follow Christ. As we come closer to Christ, we can reflect His light for our families and draw them closer to us and to Him.

1 Thomas S. Monson, "Hallmarks of a Happy Home," *Ensign*, Nov. 1988, ensign.lds.org.

Parenthood is about discipleship. If we want to raise our children to be disciples, we must be disciples ourselves. We may think parenthood is about what we want to help our children become—responsible adults firmly converted to the Lord and His gospel. But what we help our children become is only part of the equation. Parenthood is every bit as much about what we become through our parenting. President Boyd K. Packer of the Quorum of the Twelve Apostles taught, "One of the great discoveries of parenthood is that we learn far more about what really matters from our children than we ever did from our parents."[2] When our parenting choices draw us closer to Christ in our study and our actions, we may emulate the Savior in our homes and build families filled with joy and light.

Where do we begin our journey to reflect the Savior's actions in our parenting? President Dallin H. Oaks of the Quorum of the Twelve Apostles stated,

> The gospel plan each family should follow to prepare for eternal life and exaltation is outlined in the Church's 1995 proclamation, 'The Family: A Proclamation to the World.' . . . I testify that the proclamation on the family is a statement of eternal truth, the will of the Lord for His children who seek eternal life. It has been the basis of Church teaching and practice . . . and will continue so for the future. Consider it as such, teach it, live by it, and you will be blessed as you press forward toward eternal life.[3]

These are strong promises and counsel from one of the Lord's Apostles.

In the family proclamation we are taught that "successful marriages and families are established and maintained on principles of faith, prayer, repentance, forgiveness, respect, love, compassion, work, and wholesome recreational activities."[4] Studying these nine gospel principles provides a prophetic framework for parents to focus on as they seek to refine their discipleship and raise children with a desire to do likewise.

Some may have wondered about the principles that were and weren't included in this list for achieving successful families. For instance, worldly marriage and parenting experts generally extol the importance of communication as a key in maintaining healthy families. However, when the nine prophetic principles of successful families are in place, healthy communication more naturally follows. Focusing on these nine principles outlined by our modern-day prophets and

---

2 Boyd K. Packer, "And a Little Child Shall Lead Them," *Ensign*, May 2012, 8.
3 Dallin H. Oaks, "The Plan and the Proclamation," *Ensign*, Nov. 2017, 29–31.
4 "The Family: A Proclamation to the World," *Ensign*, Nov. 2010, 129.

apostles provides the blueprint families need to follow to achieve greater love and harmony at home.

Consider some examples: When parents demonstrate faith and prayer on a daily basis, children don't wonder what their parents hold dear. When family members treat each other with love, respect, and compassion, family bonds grow strong. When parents repent and forgive and teach their children to do likewise, family members can feel safe to make mistakes and continue to learn and grow. Parents must extend compassion and show love if they expect to build a home that is a haven of love, peace, and joy. As parents work to strengthen the nine principles in their own lives and purify their discipleship, greater harmony and love at home will flow more naturally.

The nine principles are listed in a sequential order. Faith is the first principle and must be the foundation of our lives. When faith is strong, prayer follows. Meaningful prayers naturally yield repentance and forgiveness as we realize our dependence on God. The next principle listed is respect; when we are firmly grounded in Christ and His doctrine, the Spirit whispers the need to respect our children and those around us. Love comes next—love flows more naturally between parents and children when everyone is treated with respect. As we live lives of faith, prayer, and repentance, our hearts are filled with God's love, and extending that love to our family members and others is the next step. When our hearts are filled with love, we treat others with compassion, the next principle. Work comes next as an essential life skill to share with children, who may have an easier time joining in the family workload when respect, love, and compassion are present. Wholesome recreational activities provide the icing on our family cake, a necessary balance for work, and a meaningful vehicle for bonding families together.

Parenting based on these nine gospel principles does not offer quick fixes, snap solutions, or a family full of perfect harmony and flawless choices. As President Howard W. Hunter taught, "Perhaps there are children who have come into the world that would challenge any set of parents under any set of circumstances."[5] Sometimes, despite the best intentions and efforts of stalwart parents, children still make grievous choices. But in your parenting dilemmas, if you study and practice basic gospel principles such as prayer, respect, love, forgiveness, and compassion, your family environment may improve. I have found in my own parenting that as I focus on the nine prophetic principles delineated in the family proclamation, the path I should take becomes clearer, and I am filled with hope and reassurance.

The chapters of this book systematically consider each of the nine principles listed in the family proclamation. Each chapter shares prophetic

5 *Teachings of Presidents of the Church: Howard W. Hunter* (2015), 228.

counsel and promises, offers specific suggestions for applying these principles in your home, and draws examples from the lives of Church leaders as well as from today's families. I have found that studying the personal lives of modern-day prophets and apostles offers hope, inspiration, and sweet examples of gospel living. Let me share one story as we begin.

The terrain of parenthood is fraught with days filled with fatigue and nights heavy with worry. All good parents have moments when they wonder if things will turn out all right for their children. No parent is alone in these concerns—all good parents have felt the same emotions and battled the same fears. On one occasion, when President David O. McKay was a boy, his mother asked him to drive away a stray cow in their pasture. David jumped onto his horse (without a saddle or bridle), chased the cow off, and then galloped up to the family's porch, "coming precariously close" to a visiting neighbor to announce that he had finished his task. Startled by David's seemingly reckless nature, the visitor shook her head and warned David's mother, "Mark my words, that boy will come to no good end!"[6]

It makes you chuckle, doesn't it? Sometimes in dark moments I like to recall that story. President David O. McKay turned out wonderfully well, despite his neighbor's dire predictions. Parenthood is hard, but we can persevere with hope and faith. If we focus on our personal discipleship and build homes firmly grounded in gospel principles, there is always hope.

As you read this book, don't overwhelm yourself and try to do everything at once. Focus on one principle for a month. The end of each chapter lists a series of application questions and suggestions. After reading a chapter, consider the application ideas. Choose one or two helpful goals to set for yourself and your family. If you are married, counsel with your spouse. Address some topics in family council. Work together as a family, and savor your successes. After a month or two of progress with one principle, choose another principle to address. Undoubtedly you are already good at many of the topics discussed in this book, but all of us have room to improve. Periodically assess how your family is doing. Reread chapters from time to time, when you need a quick crash course or new inspiration. I have noticed my own parenting methods improve when I periodically review the nine principles and work to freshly apply them in our family.

Remember that no family is perfect, and don't compare your weaknesses to others' strengths. Though not all challenges are seen by others, all families have trials and heartaches. Some deal with physical, mental, or emotional

---

6 Mary Jane Woodger, *David O. McKay: Beloved Prophet* (2004), 12.

difficulties. Sometimes spouses have a hard time reaching a consensus on faith or parenting issues. Some face parenting tests alone, without a spouse. Others deal with financial or employment challenges. Comparing your family to others isn't fair and won't ever help you feel good. Just as you cheer and celebrate your children's smallest victories, your Heavenly Father rejoices in your every effort and never compares you and your development with that of your neighbors or peers. Remember that although the stories told in this book are true, they are just a tiny glimpse into the lives of the people they portray. The people in the stories were and are real people, with strengths and flaws, just like you. While it can be helpful to focus on others' strengths, that doesn't mean they don't have weaknesses. Use the stories to inspire you and not to beat yourself up.

Do the best you can, and be patient with yourself and your progress. I like President Lorenzo Snow's thoughts: "Do not expect to become perfect at once. If you do, you will be disappointed. Be better today than you were yesterday, and be better tomorrow than you are today."[7] Set a goal, and review your progress every day when you pray. Thank the Lord for your successes. Pray for strength, and repent when you need to. Apologize to your family, and keep trying. Be humble and prayerful, and trust in the Savior's grace. The Lord has a plan for your family, and He will be with you. Over time, as you strive to consistently make Christlike choices in your parenting, your very nature can change. As Elder Richard G. Scott of the Quorum of the Twelve Apostles taught, "We *become* what we want to *be* by consistently *being* what we want to *become* each day. . . . A consistent, righteous life produces an inner power and strength that can be permanently resistant to the eroding influence of sin and transgression."[8] Through days, weeks, months, and years, the more you work to be faithful, forgiving, loving, and compassionate, the easier these choices will be as they become part of who you are. Parenting can be a beautiful, sanctifying path when you make such choices.

God bless you in your journey to focus on gospel principles, refine your personal discipleship, and lead your family to do the same.

---

7 *Teachings of Presidents of the Church: Lorenzo Snow* (2012), 103.
8 Richard G. Scott, "The Transforming Power of Faith and Character," *Ensign*, Nov. 2010, 43–44, emphases in original.

CHAPTER 1
Faith: Daily and Weekly Choices

"Do [our] children know that we love God with all our heart and that we long to see the face—and fall at the feet—of His Only Begotten Son?"
—Jeffrey R. Holland[1]

FAITH CANNOT BE A CASUAL choice in today's world. Your faith—and the faith of your children—will be tried and tested throughout life. Sometimes those tests are sent or allowed by a loving Father who wants to strengthen our faith and teach us of Him and His plan for us. Other times our faith will be openly assaulted by worldly voices that mock, deride, and cast doubt. If we hope to stand strong in this environment, our faith must be firmly grounded. If we want to raise children who can be strong and able to stand in the days before the Savior's return, we should convey our faith to our children in strong, undeniable ways and help them develop deep roots as their testimonies begin to grow.

Do your children know what you believe? Have you made it real for them through stories, experiences, and testimonies? Do they remember the truths you have shared? Have they seen the light in your eyes as you testify of the things that matter most to you? In their moments of uncertainty, can they look at your life and actions and feel complete confidence in your beliefs?

Today's parents must heed Elder Jeffrey R. Holland's plea to "live the gospel as conspicuously as you can."[2] We must make conscious daily choices that reflect our deepest-held beliefs. Our children must know our belief goes much further than social conversion, beyond a habit of going to church because it's what we were taught or because it's convenient. They must see the gospel as part of our daily lives, and they must hear what it means to us.

---

1 Jeffrey R. Holland, "A Prayer for the Children," *Ensign*, May 2003, 87.
2 Holland, "A Prayer for the Children," 86.

As our children get older, we must also invite them to come and know for themselves. We can do much to teach our children to search the doctrine, understand its applications, and liken the stories to themselves (see 1 Nephi 19:23). When our children become converted to Jesus Christ and His gospel, they will be ready to stand for Him and lead the next generation. As we establish homes where we daily rejoice in the light of Christ's doctrine, our children can know where to find truth and how to receive the answers they will need in a dark world.

There are many important ways parents can strengthen their own faith and establish homes built on faith—too many to reasonably fit in one chapter. This chapter will focus on daily and weekly choices we can make to create homes of faith. The next chapter will discuss additional ways parents can consider a long-term vision and build a family culture of faith in Jesus Christ and His gospel.

Love of Scriptures
Parental Love of Scriptures
One of the most important choices we can make is to study the scriptures every day, by ourselves, with our spouses (for those who are married), and in our families. As family members learn to feast on the scriptures, the dynamics of relationships in the home will improve. President Thomas S. Monson pleaded with us to read the Book of Mormon every day. He said, "The importance of having a firm and sure testimony of the Book of Mormon cannot be overstated."[3] President Russell M. Nelson said, "As you prayerfully study the Book of Mormon *every day,* you will make better decisions—*every day.* I promise that as you ponder what you study, the windows of heaven will open, and you will receive answers to your own questions and direction for your own life. I promise that as you daily immerse yourself in the Book of Mormon, you can be immunized against the evils of the day, even the gripping plague of pornography and other mind-numbing addictions."[4] Who wouldn't appreciate the ability to make better decisions every day and receive direction for their life? These are phenomenal blessings all of us need.

The scriptural standard we live by in our homes won't often rise above the example set by the parents. If we want our children to love and live by the word of God, we should do so ourselves. We can do much to demonstrate our love of the scriptures for our children. President James E. Faust of the

---

3 Thomas S. Monson, "The Power of the Book of Mormon," *Ensign,* May 2017, 86.
4 Russell M. Nelson, "The Book of Mormon: What Would Your Life Be Like Without It?" *Ensign,* Nov. 2017, 62–63, emphases in original.

Quorum of the Twelve Apostles fondly remembered his mother's love of the Book of Mormon and how she often taught her sons by quoting from it. He said, "No one had to tell her that one can get closer to God by reading the Book of Mormon than by any other book. She was already there."[5] Do our children know we love the scriptures? Do they see them left out, pages open and marked? Do they catch us reading them? Do they know we depend on them for strength and reassurance?

Elder Bruce R. McConkie's son reported that his father and grandfathers "did not bribe their children to read the scriptures or nag them about religious duties. They simply loved the Lord and loved the scriptures, and their children and grandchildren, who loved them, caught that spirit and sought to imitate that example."[6] If our children grow up seeing us feasting on the scriptures, they may more naturally follow that example and know where to turn for answers and guidance.

I have observed this principle at work in our own home. One October, my husband, Cameron, was at a crossroads in his scripture study and was trying to decide what to study next. After a bit of deliberation, he set a goal to start the Book of Mormon again and finish it by Christmas. Cameron and I were in a habit of waking up early and studying our scriptures together on the couch in our living room. Many mornings our children would wake up and wander in to snuggle or just be in the same room, and eventually they all heard about my husband's new scripture goal.

Every Christmas Eve our family gathers to write down gifts to Jesus—goals we would like to work on for the next year to become more Christlike. Our son was seven that Christmas season. He took a cue from my husband's recent scripture-reading achievement, and he decided that the next year he would read the Book of Mormon through from cover to cover by Christmas. The year after that, our four-year-old daughter followed her brother's example and decided to read the Book of Mormon through (with parental help) by the next Christmas. We were amazed at all the scripture reading that followed from one simple parental goal.

Effective Personal Scripture Study

In addition to silently teaching the importance of the scriptures, parental example can teach children how to study, search, and feast on the scriptures.

5 James P. Bell, *In the Strength of the Lord: The Life and Teachings of James E. Faust* (1999), 20–21.

6 Joseph Fielding McConkie, *The Bruce R. McConkie Story: Reflections of a Son* (2003), 236–37.

Studying the scriptures isn't something we learn to do once and never have to relearn. Truly feasting on the scriptures requires us to delve deeper as we study them each time and learn to ask questions. There are several different tools and a variety of study methods to make scripture study more effective.

When and Where

Effective scripture study begins with a solid commitment to try (and keep trying) to learn from the word of God. Set aside a time of day that works best for you. Some prefer early morning, waking before their families to start their day with the Spirit. Some feel more awake studying at night. Some study when their little ones are napping or when older children are at school. Schedule a time and place you can study your scriptures with minimal distractions, and be consistent. Pray to know when the best time might be. Sometimes it is helpful to set a goal for how long you would like to study each day. In some seasons of life achieving fifteen minutes of daily study would be a Herculean accomplishment, while other seasons of life are more generous. I love the sentiment of a sister in my ward who stated that when we finish reading the scriptures the Lord doesn't think, "Well, you sure didn't read for very long today!" No, the heavens cheer for us and are proud of our efforts and successes. Effective personal scripture study is a gift you give yourself and your family—the doctrinal moorings, Spirit, and peace you gain from scripture study pay dividends to both.

Tools

Many people enjoy marking their scriptures, making notes in the margins, and highlighting significant verses. One of my friends enjoys illustrating her scriptures—drawing images of key words in the margins to help her better visualize the passage. A good red marking pencil or other colored pencils can do wonders here. Pick up an inexpensive copy of the Book of Mormon and mark only passages that teach about a topic of your choice, such as faith, covenants, or charity. Buy an inexpensive copy of the New Testament and mark passages with Christ's miracles or parables. One of the most inspirational studies I have completed is marking each Book of Mormon prophet's words and experiences in a different color. (This required me to pick up a set of twenty-four colored pencils, and some of the prophets were marked in combinations of two colors so I had enough colors.) Doing this gave me powerful insights into the individual testimonies of each prophet and deepened my love for their personal sacrifices and contributions.

You may also find that choosing a notebook as a scripture journal helps. If you set a goal to record at least one thought or insight from your study each day, you will be motivated to sit up, pay attention, and ask questions about what you read. The more you ponder and record your thoughts, the more discoveries you will make.

STUDY METHODS

It helps to vary how you study the scriptures from time to time. Sometimes it works best to choose a standard work and read it straight through, making notes and drawing inspiration as you go. Other times you might drum up a list of questions or topics you would like to study further. You can choose one particular topic, take a few months to study it deeply, and write a paper or talk about it. Scripture study is a lifetime endeavor and requires us to study and restudy in whatever way works best as we keep learning and applying scriptural truths in our lives.

One of the most formative scripture study experiences of my life took place during my freshman year at BYU when I took an honors English class in conjunction with an honors Book of Mormon class. I was assigned to spend the semester studying the Atonement of Jesus Christ and to write several small papers and a longer term paper on my doctrinal discoveries. During those months of studying, analyzing, and writing about the relationships of justification, sanctification, the Fall, and Christlike attributes to Jesus Christ's Atonement, my life was changed forever. Many times in the ensuing years I have drawn on those wells of doctrinal understanding for strength and comfort.

How might studying the doctrine of the Atonement of Jesus Christ revitalize your discipleship and your parenting?

As parents drink deeply from the doctrine in the scriptures, they will be prepared to share those truths with their children. When parents know and love the scriptures, they can teach their children the stories in a way that brings scripture heroes to life. They can show their children how the scriptures provide guidance and counsel in life's challenges. Parental love of the scriptures may naturally trickle down as parents set the example.

Family Scripture Study

When parents' love of scriptures is deeply rooted, quality family scripture study will likely follow. We can choose to gather our children around us to feast on the scriptures each day. And from their early childhood we can fill their hearts and minds with scripture stories.

When President Gordon B. Hinckley was growing up, his mother would gather the children around the stove before bed and read a book called *Mother Stories from the Book of Mormon*. This early introduction sparked an interest in scripture heroes long before he learned to read the scriptures directly.[7]

President Joseph Fielding Smith inculcated a love of scripture stories into his family culture through dramatic retelling of scripture stories for his family at breakfast. "The suspense I felt wondering if Pharaoh's soldiers would find the gold cup in Benjamin's sack of grain is real even today," his daughter said. "Today his teachings . . . lift and sustain his descendants. . . . What a great privilege and blessing it has been to be his daughter."[8]

In 3 Nephi 17, parents brought their children to the feet of the Savior, and the Savior individually blessed and prayed for each child. I have wondered what it would have felt like to be there for that glorious manifestation. I cannot travel in time to be there, and I can't physically bring my children to the Savior. But I can do my best to spiritually bring them to Christ. I can tell my children about Christ's miracles. I can witness of His birth, His ministry, His teachings, and His miracles. I can testify of His Resurrection and what that means for each of us. I can pour my soul into helping my children know Christ from infancy by the stories and testimony I share.

When our children were small, I fell into a habit of regaling them with scripture hero stories at bedtime. With the lights turned out and the kids all snuggled under their blankets, I loved to bring the stories of Daniel, David, Ammon, Nephi, Alma, Abinadi, and others to life. At times I compiled lists of which stories I wanted to tell them so I didn't forget any.

The scriptures are a treasury of miracles, healings, and dramatic manifestations that were granted through faith and righteousness. Sharing those stories with our children will help their testimonies grow.

Is there a time of day—over the breakfast table, at bedtime, or in some other time slot—when you could conveniently slip in a few scripture hero stories or share the nuggets of inspiration you have gleaned from your recent studies?

In addition to actively and consistently sharing scripture stories with our children, it is essential for parents to hold daily family scripture study. Admittedly, this is no small task. I have often pondered this counsel from Margaret D. Nadauld, former Young Women general president and mother of seven sons: "It's not always easy to get children in a mood to join the family in scripture reading. Remember to keep it happy, keep it light. Serious times

---

7 Sheri L. Dew, *Go Forward with Faith: The Biography of Gordon B. Hinckley* (1996), 34.

8 *Teachings of Presidents of the Church: Joseph Fielding Smith* (2013), 205.

come soon enough."[9] When parents are truly converted to the importance of scripture study, they may at times feel tempted to try to compel family members to join them. Family scripture study, like other aspects of parenting, must be handled "only by persuasion, by long-suffering, by gentleness and meekness, and by love unfeigned" (D&C 121:41). If children are joining family scripture study by choice—by loving invitation—it will be much easier for them to feel the Spirit and soak in scriptural doctrine. Do the best you can to form a family habit. Counsel with your family about when scripture study together could best be accomplished. Pray for guidance and wisdom. Then follow through consistently, and invite children to participate in a spirit of love. Often through the years we have coaxed our children out of bed for morning scripture study by tickling them or singing to them or have carried them to the living room with piggyback rides. On occasion, when someone has really felt contrary, we have knelt around their bed for morning prayer and scripture study.

Like personal scripture study, family scripture study may need to be readdressed and changed from time to time. When our children were small, we started reading a column out of the Book of Mormon every morning during breakfast. We reasoned that their mouths were full, and they were quiet and would listen while we read, explained, and discussed. This worked well for a couple of years. After that we counseled together as a family and moved scripture study to the living room right before breakfast. We liked to read a page, sing a hymn, and pray together. After a few more years Cameron's employment changed, and we again found ourselves reading at the table before he and some of our children hurried out the door. Sometimes people are tired or don't want to read, and we do our best to lovingly encourage. Some mornings we are too far behind, and we end up reading scriptures at night. We do the best we can to be consistent and show our children the importance of scripture study.

Each family must decide what works for them. Some families read in the morning. Some families listen to the scriptures in the car. Some families read verses during dinner or before bed. One dear friend who is a single parent shared that she likes to send her children to bed with the scriptures in their heads. At the end of the day she invites her children to all snuggle together in her bed while they read scriptures (and sometimes a story from the *Friend*), pray, and hug each other right before bed. She admits that with small children there are still lots of crazy moments sandwiched in with all that cuddling. But at the end of a sometimes hectic day, she likes sending her children to bed with love.

9 Margaret D. Nadauld, *A Mother's Influence* (2004), 40.

When children are young, you can begin by helping them repeat a verse in phrases one at a time. As children get older they can participate by each reading a verse or two. Some families encourage everyone to bring their scriptures to mark and discuss together. One faithful mother I know would occasionally misread a word and offered a dollar to any teenage son who could catch her error. This twist made scripture reading new and exciting. The children listened more attentively, and finding the error became a fun game. Some families encourage each member to find a verse or principle that applies to them each day during family study. One family I know recites a verse together every day until every child has passed it off, and when each child passes it off they put money in their future mission account. Another family I know supplements their family scripture study with Bible videos by The Church of Jesus Christ of Latter-day Saints to bring stories to life and keep different age groups engaged. Another friend has a husband who has gone through periods of church activity and inactivity and isn't supportive of family scripture study. Eventually my friend decided she would study scriptures with her children during breakfast after her husband left for work. There are endless ways to involve family members and encourage active participation in scripture study. Pray about it, counsel together as much as you can, and choose what works best for you at this time in your life. Then do it!

Through the ups, downs, and endless effort of scripture study, remember that consistency is key. Not every day will be a stunning success. Some days you will want to throw in the towel. But as you work consistently over time, your love and testimony of the scriptures can seep through to your children's hearts. I love the principle shared by Elder David A. Bednar of the Quorum of the Twelve Apostles. He explained that when their three boys were growing up, their family scripture study efforts were occasionally interrupted by "outbursts such as 'He's touching me!' 'Make him stop looking at me!' 'Mom, he's breathing my air!'" Sounds pretty familiar to most parents, doesn't it? Elder Bednar admitted that he and his wife would sometimes feel frustrated and wonder if their efforts to teach their children were accomplishing any good. He said, "Today if you could ask our adult sons what they remember about family prayer, scripture study, and family home evening, . . . what they would say they remember is that as a family we were consistent. . . . The consistency of our intent and work was perhaps the greatest lesson—a lesson we did not fully appreciate at the time."[10]

Family scripture study is work, and it requires consistent, concerted effort. But in that work parents lay a tremendous foundation for their families

10 David A. Bednar, "More Diligent and Concerned at Home," *Ensign*, Nov. 2009, 19.

and instill the faith they hope will be passed on to their grandchildren and great-grandchildren.

Helping Children Partake

In addition to holding family scripture study, parents must teach their children to search the doctrine, know for themselves, and love the Lord with all their hearts.

Have you ever thought about the problems that are solved as people come to Christ with deep resolve and pure hearts? As we fervently seek after Christ through personal worship and life choices, our hearts are purified. It is easier to love ourselves and those around us. We discover hope, confidence, and peace. Personalities mellow as we are filled with God's love and our lives begin to reflect Christlike attributes. Wouldn't these be wonderful events to have happen in our children's lives?

Truly, the solution to many of our parental worries is to help our children know and deeply love the Lord. As we lead our children to Christ, they can begin to feel His love and peace. Christlike virtues and choices can begin to take root in their hearts. They will feel more confident and hopeful. As they grow and encounter difficulties and challenges, they will know where to turn for the answers they need. Beautiful things can happen in our children's lives as they learn to love and follow the Lord Jesus Christ. Helping children establish habits of personal scripture study is a critical step in their conversion.

Parents can do much to teach their children to drink from the fount of truth. Show your children how the scriptures provide answers to your challenges. Help your children turn to the scriptures for answers to their own questions. Your testimony probably did not arrive all in one day, and the same will be true for your children. Just as you paid a price of diligent study and inquiry to know the truthfulness of the gospel, your children must put forth effort to become converted. Youth must be prepared to stand for their faith, and parents can prepare them to do this by surrounding them with and teaching them how to search for scriptural truths.

It is important to remember that scripture study is a skill that requires practice and patience, and parents can do much to help their children get started. Sit down with your child and discuss topics they are interested in studying. What doctrinal questions do they have? When children reach an appropriate age and as they show interest, teach them how to mark their scriptures. If you individually read a bit of scripture to a young child before bed, you can discuss what you're reading together or invite your child to speak up when they hear a verse they would like to mark. Discuss key verses together. Teaching children to mark their scriptures and keep a scripture journal introduces them to the glorious doctrinal understandings that only come as we search, study, and actively engage in our scriptures.

One of my friends and her husband help each of their children set a goal to read the Book of Mormon through before they are baptized. Starting when each child turns six, they are given a hardcover copy of the Book of Mormon, and the parents help them begin reading it. In the beginning they may read only a couple of verses each day. As the child gets older, they slowly progress to reading more. As their baptism date approaches, the parents help their children chart a course to finish their goal in time for their special day. I love this personalized method of introducing each child to the Book of Mormon and helping them begin to gain a testimony of it at such a young age.

Family scripture study provides an ideal setting for gospel discussion and asking and answering questions that will assist your children in their road to conversion. As you read together, ask questions to see what your children understand. Probe for your children's thoughts and feelings about verses they read or chapters the family covers. Look for specific doctrines, values, or attributes to discuss. If your child has a question about a verse or concept, don't be afraid to derail your previous reading to discuss their concerns.

When President Harold B. Lee's daughters were growing up, if they had a question or were preparing a talk, they would ask their father what he thought. He would respond by inviting them to each get out their scriptures to see what the Lord said. With each person's scriptures open, they would search for doctrinal answers together. It was years later before one of his daughters realized all her father was accomplishing through this ritual. Of the experience she said,

> He taught us that the scriptures were where we turn first for our answers. He didn't go to the intellectual, academic, or philosophical answers of men. . . . Those, he told us, were wonderful resources, but they were sought only after we had searched the scriptures and the spiritual essence was understood. These were keys to his profound knowledge of the scriptures, and he wanted us to know and love them, too.[11]

Teaching children how to study their scriptures is an incredible gift with eternal dividends. As your children learn to love and study God's word, they may draw closer to their Heavenly Father and Savior and find the peace

---

11 L. Brent Goates, *Harold B. Lee: Prophet and Seer* (1985), 122.

and happiness they need to conquer life's challenges and return to their heavenly home.

Sabbath Observance

In addition to developing a love of scriptures, creating a family culture of Sabbath observance builds faith and fortifies family members. The King James Bible Dictionary shares a significant insight about the Sabbath: "The importance of a sacred day for man to rest from his temporal labors, contemplate the word of the Lord, and assemble for public worship is a major item in a person's spiritual development. Furthermore, a decay in the national religious life always follows any tendency toward carelessness in the matter of Sabbath observance" (Bible Dictionary, "Sabbath").

Those are significant statements. Keeping the Sabbath is of major importance in a child's spiritual development. If lacking Sabbath observance creates decreasing religious devotion in a nation, it is possible a lack of Sabbath training for our children may result in lacking spirituality throughout their lives. Is it possible we don't fully comprehend the importance of making the Sabbath day holy, both for ourselves and for our children?

In Exodus 31:13–14 the Lord states: "Verily my sabbaths ye shall keep: for it is a sign between me and you throughout your generations; that ye may know that I am the Lord that doth sanctify you. Ye shall keep the sabbath therefore; for it is holy unto you." Here the Lord reminds us both that the Sabbath is holy and that the Lord is the one who sanctifies us, or makes us holy. Striving for a more holy, spiritually uplifting Sabbath in our families can make us a more holy, sanctified people. The choices we make on the Sabbath can be signs of love to our Heavenly Father.[12] The Sabbath is to be a day of rest, but it is also a day of worship, a day of holiness. When choosing activities, consider how worshipful they are. Does the activity bring you closer to the Lord? Does it strengthen your family's relationships? Does it help your children love the Lord and His gospel more deeply?

Creating a happy, reverent Sabbath atmosphere in our homes takes concerted effort. I like to set the tone in our home with reverent music on Sunday morning. Over breakfast or lunch we like to discuss which Sabbath activities each family member would like to choose for the day. If your children are young, having a list with a few options is helpful. Keep things moving, and choose activities that can be done in manageable bits that respect a child's attention span and interests.

---

12 Russell M. Nelson, "The Sabbath Is a Delight," *Ensign*, May 2015, 130.

Sabbath Scripture Activities

Parents can gather their children on Sunday mornings to read from the scriptures and tell scripture stories. There are many ways to make Sabbath scriptural retellings and reenactments special and enjoyable. We have a little bag of items that are mentioned in the scriptures—simple things such as wheat kernels, corn kernels, a cut-out paper or fabric sun, a rock, a boat, a coin, a tithing envelope, and a sheep or other plastic animal. Sometimes at Sunday breakfast we will pull out the bag, take out an item, and let everyone guess what that item has to do with the scriptures. Then we will look up appropriate scriptures and explain principles or parables.

If you would like to have a family scripture bag, choose a simple bag and keep your eyes open for small trinkets you can add—a tiny treasure chest or toy sword, a bar of soap, a stick, a heart, a candle, or a small metal rod. With a little thought and searching you can pull a good assortment of items together without much difficulty. It helps to have a list of topics and scriptures that match each item. You can either put each item in its own clear plastic bag with a paper listing appropriate scriptures and principles, or you can keep a master list in the scripture bag that includes possible scripture references and stories for each item.

Another scriptural activity we have chosen is scripture charades. When our children were young we would pull out a few scripture pictures we had cut out from Church magazines. Spreading them out on display we would invite our kids to choose a story to act out and then let us guess. Another simple variation is drawing scripture stories to guess instead of acting them out. Make a list of scripture stories, let family members take turns drawing a story or gospel principle, and see how long it takes the rest of the family to guess what the drawing represents.

Another entertaining scripture game is for each family member to attach a sticky note or a card listing a person or place from the scriptures to his or her forehead with a bandana. All other family members can see the card and answer the person's questions until the person can guess the scripture item on his or her forehead. Going around the circle, each person takes turns asking a question about the item on his or her card until everyone has guessed correctly. Through the years we have loved these Sunday antics that teach but also entertain.

If our children get restless, Cameron often takes them to build the city of Jerusalem or Zarahemla in the sandbox or to build a train track to take the pioneers to Utah. (You could accomplish similar objectives with block temple constructions.) One year he invented a game he called "Prophet Tag." With our children in the backyard he tosses a ball to a child and names a prophet (either modern or ancient). The person who gets the ball has to name another prophet before passing the ball on. Activities like these respect children's need for movement while still recognizing the Sabbath. I often remember the following counsel from President Gordon B. Hinckley when I am trying to balance my children's need for activity with Sabbath observance: "Now I do not want to be prudish. I do not want you to lock your children in the house and read the Bible all afternoon to them. Be wise. Be careful. But make that day a day when you can sit down with your families and talk about sacred and good things."[13] Parents must respect their children's developmental needs and not make the Sabbath a day that they will dread. The ultimate goal is to make the Sabbath a day of rest for the family, a day consciously set apart with different activities than other days of the week.

Family History Activities

The Sabbath also provides priceless opportunities to engage our families in family history work. Elder David A. Bednar has promised that youth who become involved in family history will feel greater love for their ancestors, a greater testimony of Christ, and greater protection against the adversary. (Wouldn't you love those blessings for your children? I would!) Further, he pleaded with parents to "please help your children and youth to learn about and experience the Spirit of Elijah. But do not overly program this endeavor or provide too much detailed information or training. Invite young people to explore, to experiment, and to learn for themselves."[14]

Exposure to family history can begin when children are young. Get a poster board, sit down with your children on a Sunday afternoon, and map out your family tree. Ideally this can take weeks to complete. As you add each new member's name, tell stories about that ancestor, show pictures, and identify birthdays. Help your children relate to their ancestors' lives.

Another fun Sunday afternoon activity can be showing your children relativefinder.org. This BYU-sponsored website allows members to sign in using their Family Search account. After you sign in the site will give you a list of prophets, movie stars, politicians, musical composers, and others you are related to. You may be surprised at who all your relatives are.

You can also begin to share family history with young children through compiling a book of stories about your ancestors. Interview relatives and gather a variety of stories—conversion or faith-promoting stories and others

---

13 Gordon B. Hinckley, *Teachings of Gordon B. Hinckley* (1997), 559–60.
14 David A. Bednar, "The Hearts of the Children Shall Turn," *Ensign*, Nov. 2011, 27.

children would enjoy. At our home we have a book of grandparents' bedtime stories. These stories are written at a child's level and include drawings, pictures, recipes, and stories about ancestors. Some of them are stories of faith—conversion and missionary stories. Others are simple stories they can relate to, like the time their great-grandfather ate too much ice cream on his birthday and discovered you can have too much of a good thing. Through the years our children have often pulled out these ancestor stories, and the favorites get reread a lot. Taking advantage of time on the Sabbath to share stories and pictures is a beautiful way to give young children a sense of heritage and belonging.

As children grow, family history time can naturally expand to include indexing and researching personal ancestors for temple work. Sit down with your older children and introduce them to Family Search. Teach them how to index, and show them their family tree. If they have grown up listening to stories and seeing pictures of ancestors, this may be a smoother transition than it would be if their first introduction to family history occurs when they are older. The spirit of Elijah is powerful and can be a tremendous force for good in the lives of our youth.

How can you use family history activities to strengthen the faith of your children?

Creating a joyful family atmosphere of worship and love on the Sabbath can help inoculate our families against the worldly trends that surround us and deepen our children's love for Christ and His gospel.[15]

Family Home Evening

Another critical way to share our faith with our children is through family home evening. When the family home evening principle was first introduced by President Joseph F. Smith in 1915, he said, "If the Saints obey this counsel, we promise that great blessings will result. Love at home and obedience to parents will increase. Faith will be developed in the hearts of the youth of Israel, and they will gain power to combat the evil influence and temptations which beset them."[16] As with so many other gospel principles, these are valuable promises for our families.

When the family home evening program was introduced, Presidents Ezra Taft Benson and Gordon B. Hinckley were still in their youth. George Benson, President Benson's father, announced to his family, "The Presidency

---

15 For extra Sabbath ideas, I love *Celebrate Sunday* by Lani Olsen Hilton. It is packed with inventive ways to keep the Sabbath enjoyable for family members of all ages.

16 *Teachings of Presidents of the Church: Joseph F. Smith* (1998), 348.

has spoken, and this is the word of the Lord to us." After that day the Benson family observed a weekly home evening.[17] Similarly, President Hinckley's parents announced that they would be having family night once a week, and they did.[18]

In announcing their determination to be obedient to the prophet and then following through, the heads of the Benson and Hinckley families sent a strong message of faith and faithfulness to their children. Later in life their children chose to embrace the faith their parents sought to share in this weekly ritual. In our families today we have the opportunity to send the same strong message to our children of obedience to prophetic counsel.

Holding weekly family home evenings requires a solid commitment from parents, along with fortitude and determination to follow through week after week. In some seasons of life this may require flexibility or sacrifice. Consider the following quote from Elder Richard G. Scott: "Be cautious not to make your family home evening just an afterthought of a busy day. Decide that on Monday night your family will be together at home for the evening. Do not let employment demands, sports, extracurricular activities, homework, or anything else become more important than that time you spend together at home with your family."[19] Sometimes keeping Monday night set apart may require sacrificing some activities. Perhaps, at times, critical demands may require moving family night to another night. Some parents may not support a typical family home evening, and couples or co-parents in these situations will need to counsel together to decide what form family night will take in their home. Are there mutually held values that could be shared in lessons? Or would one parent be more supportive of a night on which the family simply played and enjoyed each other? Prayerfully consider how to best hold family night in your home.

In addition to scheduling and planning difficulties, holding weekly family night often requires parents to cheerfully press forward despite behavior or attitude problems among their children. When President Gordon B. Hinckley's parents announced their commitment to hold a weekly family night, the children did not automatically fall into line. President Hinckley remembered moans and groans, smirks and guffaws. "It must have been disgusting to my parents the way we giggled," he recalled. But he also saw how family night

---

17 Sheri L. Dew, *Ezra Taft Benson: A Biography* (1987), 25.

18 Sheri L. Dew, *Go Forward with Faith: The Biography of Gordon B. Hinckley* (1996), 34.

19 Richard G. Scott, "Make the Exercise of Faith Your First Priority," *Ensign*, Nov. 2014, 94.

helped their family grow closer to each other and become united in gospel truths.[20]

When Patricia Pinegar, a former Primary general president, and her husband were raising their eight children, family home evening was sometimes challenging. One particular evening the kids were restless and kept wondering aloud when it would be over. Finally their mom broke down and cried. Their daughter Kelly remembers, "Mom was frustrated, but she never gave up on us. We kept having family home evening every Monday, and today we feel like we are a forever family."[21]

That is a helpful perspective to consider. Often, as we go through the daily motions of parenting, it is easy to wonder if our actions make any difference. Parents of babies and toddlers may wonder why they go to church only to walk the halls with a fussy little one. Other times we wonder if efforts for family scripture study, prayer, and family night have any positive effect. Elder David A. Bednar observed, "Each family prayer, each episode of family scripture study, and each family home evening is a brush stroke on the canvas of our souls. No one event may appear to be very impressive or memorable. But . . . our consistency in doing seemingly small things can lead to significant spiritual results."[22] As parents keep trying day after day, week after week, and year after year, children can receive the intended message of faith and testimony. Over time those parents' actions are consecrated for their gain, and children may reflect the faith that was diligently taught them for so long.

As soon as children are old enough to participate, give them active roles each week in family night. Individual assignments give family members responsibility and help them feel ownership. You can have as many or as few assignments as you need—one family I know even puts one child in charge of sharing a family history moment and serving as the family historian to keep the minutes for the week. Involving children in lessons, scriptures, prayers, and family history moments also allows parents to see what their children know and understand. For instance, years ago we had a Sullivan family missionary training center (MTC) series for several family night lessons. We taught our kids about missions, let them put on our old missionary nametags, and sent them out on our front porch to knock on our door as "missionaries." We would welcome them in and pretend to be investigators, asking them

20 Dew, *Go Forward with Faith*, 34.
21 Janet Peterson and LaRene Gaunt, *The Children's Friends: Primary Presidents and Their Lives of Service* (1996), 176–177.
22 David A. Bednar, "More Diligent and Concerned at Home," *Ensign*, Nov. 2009, 19–20.

questions and letting them teach us. In the process we gained helpful insights into our children's current doctrinal understandings.

In addition to helping parents understand a child's testimony, family night provides an ideal setting for teaching values that might need more emphasis. Some of the topics we have covered through the years include the following:

- A series of lessons focusing on the doctrine taught in the family proclamation
- A missionary series covering basic doctrine and other important pre-missionary topics
- A pre-baptism series including basic gospel doctrine and the importance of covenants, baptism, confirmation, and the sacrament
- A series of lessons leading up to Easter, focusing on the life of Christ
- A series of lessons teaching about different ancestors, their experiences, and their faith
- A review of a different general conference talk each week with fun biographical details about the speaker found on lds.org
- A series of lessons focusing on the Restoration and the priesthood
- A series of lessons leading up to Christmas, focusing on different members of the nativity story
- A series focusing on scripture hero stories from different standard works
- Lessons based on a value our family is currently trying to emphasize, such as integrity, gratitude, forgiveness, repentance, or obedience
- A series of lessons on *For the Strength of Youth* standards
- An occasional lesson discussing what pornography is and what to do if you are exposed to it (The Church website overcomingpornography.org has great lesson outlines and videos for this topic.)

When parents make a commitment to hold weekly family home evenings, they make a strong statement about their faith. Similarly they send a message that family matters and that they want to be with their children. Family nights provide one more opportunity to teach your children they are valuable and that sharing your testimony with them is important to you. You build a forever family one dinner, one prayer, one family night, and one day at a time.

Serving in Church Callings

There is another way we can demonstrate our faith to our children on a daily and weekly basis, and that is how we serve in our Church callings. The Church is unique in world religions because of the many opportunities members have to strengthen their faith and to serve, whether by donating tithing, offering missionary service, or fulfilling callings. These responsibilities are often time-consuming and demanding, and sometimes it is hard for parents to juggle them with the needs of their family.

Have you ever stopped to wonder why callings are so important? There are many reasons that could quickly become apparent. The Church has lay ministry, so everyone needs to help. Callings give us a sense of belonging and help us get to know people. Callings teach us as we study doctrine and prepare lessons. Callings fill us with love as we learn of needs and reach out to serve. But I think there is at least one other reason callings are important. In *Lectures on Faith*, we read that "a religion that does not require the sacrifice of all things never has the power sufficient to produce the faith necessary unto life and salvation."[23] Sacrificing our time and means to serve in our callings strengthens our faith and sanctifies our souls. Giving that service willingly conveys a powerful, silent message to our children.

Marjorie Hinckley's daughter remembered coming home from school to find her mother's Relief Society lesson plans spread across the dining room table. Her excitement for her subject material was contagious. "I shuffled through her notes and posters and I absorbed it all. Most of all, I absorbed in a deep, deep place her love of Church work."[24]

Interestingly, a generation earlier, Marjorie had seen this same love of Church service reflected in the lives of her own parents. When her father would come home from an evening of service as a Mutual Improvement Association (Young Men's) president, he and Marjorie's mother would talk and laugh about the evening's events. When Marjorie's father served as patriarch, her mother kept the house ready for guests and always seemed her happiest when people came for blessings. Marjorie recalled, "Mother had taught us by example that the most wonderful thing in the world is to have a husband who loves the Lord. It wasn't that she ever openly said this; it was her ever constant attitude. There is nothing so powerful in the world as the example of a righteous mother."[25]

---

23 *Lectures on Faith* 6:7 (1985), 69.
24 *Glimpses into the Life and Heart of Marjorie Pay Hinckley,* ed. Virginia H. Pearce (1999), 30.
25 *Glimpses into the Life and Heart of Marjorie Pay Hinckley,* 260–61.

It is important to pause occasionally and consider how your current calling can be a blessing to your family and what your attitude about callings conveys to your children. If children grow up in a home where their parents faithfully care for the people they minister to, the children may learn about love and watchcare. If children grow up in a home where they see their parents putting time and thought into lesson plans, they may learn that the gospel is exciting and fulfilling. If children grow up in a home where the parents do not murmur when callings require uncomfortable levels of sacrifice, they can witness the beauty of sanctification through service. When parents testify of the blessings such service provides them, children may learn that callings are gifts from God.

How might you share the blessings of your calling with your children?

If you are a teacher, it is easy to discuss the things you are studying as you prepare for your lesson. During dinner on Sunday tell your family how your lesson went and what your favorite parts were. Elder L. Tom Perry of the Quorum of the Twelve Apostles remembered his mother practicing her lessons on her family. "We, of course, received the unabridged versions," he said.[26]

If you serve in a calling that provides the opportunity for you to minister to others, could your children be involved in taking those families meals or serving them in other ways? Might you share experiences you have as you serve and grow in the kingdom?

Sometimes blessings from Church service can also come in unexpected ways. President Heber J. Grant fondly remembered the years his mother served as ward Relief Society president. The calling "brought him into contact with Emmeline B. Wells, Eliza R. Snow, Zina D. Young," and other influential Relief Society leaders, some of whom had personally known the Prophet Joseph Smith. Heber loved hearing their testimonies.[27] As our children rub shoulders with the people we serve with, they may witness testimony reflected in the lives of others beyond their own families. Callings may require sacrifice, but they also provide countless blessings for families.

Sharing your faith with your children and helping them develop their own faith is the quest of a lifetime for parents. The daily and weekly choices that will begin to build that foundation of faith for your children require both time and a rock-solid commitment to keep at it when life is hard, when your children are uncooperative, and when you feel like burying your head in your pillow. But the example of parents with undaunted faith is exactly what the children of today need. President Gordon B. Hinckley pleaded with parents, "We call upon parents to devote their best efforts to the teaching and

---

26 L. Tom Perry, "Mothers Teaching Children in the Home," *Ensign*, May 2010, 30.
27 Matthew J. Haslam, *Heber J. Grant: Exemplar to the Saints* (2003), 32.

rearing of their children in gospel principles which will keep them close to the Church. The home is the basis of a righteous life, and no other instrumentality can take its place or fulfill its essential functions in carrying forward this God-given responsibility."[28]

May we as parents all rise to this divine responsibility!

Application

1. Choose a regular time to tell scripture stories to your kids. Make a list of favorites for easy reference.
2. Counsel with your family and choose the best time for family scripture study. Set a family goal to be consistent—and celebrate when you are.
3. If your children are older, look for opportunities to teach them to search the scriptures for answers. Teach them to mark their scriptures and keep a scripture journal of insights and impressions.
4. Counsel together as a family and compile a list of worshipful Sabbath activities everyone enjoys. Consider scripture guessing games like charades, drawing scripture scenes, or starting a scripture bag.
5. Compile a list of family history stories to share with your family.
6. Teach older children to index and research ancestors.
7. Set a goal to hold consistent family home evenings.
8. Develop a rotation system for family members to have family night assignments each week.
9. Consider ways your current calling might bless your family. How can you share the joy of Church service with your children?

---

28 *Teachings of Presidents of the Church: Gordon B. Hinckley* (2016), 168.

CHAPTER 2
Faith: Creating a Family Culture

The more surely you rear your children in the ways of the gospel of Jesus Christ, with love and high expectation, the more likely that there will be peace in their lives.
—*Gordon B. Hinckley*[1]

WHEN PARENTS DECIDE TO PRIORITIZE the teaching of faith in the home through scripture study, family home evening, Sabbath observance, and Church service, they lay the groundwork for a home built on faith and love. But there is still much more parents can do to prepare their children for lives of faithfulness. Consider a few basics such as tithing, baptism, temple attendance, and missionary service. What can you do to plant these doctrines deep in your children's hearts? We will discuss some ideas in this chapter.

Gospel Art and Conversations
What Do Your Walls Teach?
Let's start this chapter by pausing for a moment. Elder Gary E. Stevenson of the Quorum of the Twelve Apostles once heard Elder Glen Jenson of the Seventy recommend that members occasionally take a virtual tour of their own home. Inspired by this idea, Elder Stevenson taught, "Imagine that you are opening your front door and walking inside your home. What do you see, and how do you feel? Is it a place of love, peace, and refuge from the world, as is the temple? Is it clean and orderly? As you walk through the rooms of your home, do you see uplifting images which include appropriate pictures of the temple and the Savior?"[2] From time to time I like to take stock of what is on the walls of my home. What does the artwork we have chosen tell people about what we hold most dear? Would a visitor to our home easily detect our faith? The artwork that sends messages to a guest also sends messages to our

1 *Teachings of Presidents of the Church: Gordon B. Hinckley* (2016), 169.
2 Gary E. Stevenson, "Sacred Homes, Sacred Temples," *Ensign, May 2009, 102.*

children about the values we cherish. Home decorations are a silent way of sharing our faith with our children and others.

Marjorie Hinckley recalled a picture of the Savior that hung in her bedroom throughout her childhood. "Every morning when I woke up, the first thing I saw was the beautiful face of Jesus Christ. I was grown and long gone from home before I realized what an impact that had on me."[3]

President David O. McKay was similarly affected by chosen artwork. In the meetinghouse where he attended church in his youth hung a large picture of President John Taylor. Under the photo were the words, *The Kingdom of God or Nothing*. When church started to seem a bit long and his mind wandered, David's eyes would often rest on that picture and phrase, and it made a profound impact on him.[4]

When former Relief Society general president Bonnie Parkin was raising their boys, she kept a scripture reflecting her faith and determination to serve the Lord on the fridge. Later one of her sons told her, "I was in and out of the fridge a lot, and I knew that you and Dad meant that."[5]

Through the years different prophets have offered advice about how members can take advantage of silent opportunities to teach their children. President Howard W. Hunter counseled parents, "Keep a picture of a temple in your home that your children may see it. Teach them about the purposes of the house of the Lord. Have them plan from their earliest years to go there and to remain worthy of that blessing."[6] President Spencer W. Kimball gave another piece of advice to parents in this regard, noting that "every boy should have a picture of the prophet [Joseph Smith] in his bedroom." He explained that parents can use the picture to teach their sons to emulate Joseph Smith's character traits. He went on, "It works. . . . That's what my mother did. You couldn't have convinced her otherwise."[7] When decorating a nursery or a child's bedroom, include a picture of the Savior and a picture of the temple. Artwork gives a child's mind something to rest on, and it is wonderful when the chosen artwork has an intended purpose.

One of my friends collects statues of the Savior. When her family went to the Holy Land, each child picked out a statue of Jesus to take home to

3 Sheri L. Dew, *Go Forward with Faith: The Biography of Gordon B. Hinckley* (1996), 113.

4 Mary Jane Woodger, *David O. McKay: Beloved Prophet* (2004), 10.

5 Janet Peterson and LaRene Gaunt, *Faith, Hope, and Charity: Inspiration from the Lives of General Relief Society Presidents* (2008), 284.

6 Howard W. Hunter, "Exceeding Great and Precious Promises," *Ensign*, Nov. 1994, 8.

7 Francis M. Gibbons, *Spencer W. Kimball: Resolute Disciple, Prophet of God* (1995), 16.

help them remember their trip and what they learned and felt. These visual reminders teach and encourage faith in their home.

Another friend prints some of the inspiring things her children have said about courage, perseverance, or other values and uses these to decorate her home. Seeing the things they have said reminds her children of their own strength and commitment and encourages other family members as well.

Gospel-centered conversations naturally flow from gospel-themed artwork and enable parents to share in relaxed moments what they hold dear. Pictures provide a baby's first introduction to who Jesus is and how much He loves us. Temple artwork allows parents to teach children that their family began in the temple and to testify that because of the temple they can be together eternally. Parents can point to the temple and talk to their children about the marriages and families they may one day have. Gospel artwork gives parents opportunities to teach gospel stories and bring them to life.

In addition to pictures depicting gospel topics or stories, parents can choose décor with specific messages, such as a family motto, favorite scriptures, or cherished values. As children grow they may absorb these messages and their parents' faith. What do your walls silently teach your children?

Years ago I raised a question with Cameron: In thirty years, what do we want our children's lives to look like? What values do we hope they will embrace and reflect? We discussed and debated back and forth on this topic for several months. At the end of the process, we outlined twelve specific values we wanted to particularly emphasize in our home. Because there were twelve of them we chose to consciously celebrate one principle each month. Each of these principles hangs on an individual frame in our stairway. The value we are celebrating in the current month hangs near our kitchen table. As much as we try to actively discuss these ideas with our children, the walls provide additional silent reminders.

Incorporating Gospel Conversations into Daily Life

In addition to gospel conversations naturally springing from chosen artwork and home decorations, parents should be vigilant for opportunities to share their faith in context of life's events. Some of these may be planned events, and others may require an awareness of spontaneous opportunities. Parents may need to pray for awareness of occasions to share and touch the heart of a child. When gospel truths are written in our hearts, sharing gospel concepts in the moment flows more naturally.

During family meals share a faith-promoting experience you've had or an impression from the Spirit. Discuss gospel truths and how they play out in your daily life—the importance of integrity, how gratitude lifts your soul, or how faith sustains you through trials. Openly sharing in this way can teach children that the Lord is with us and constantly blessing us and that we must open our eyes to recognize it. You might challenge your family to an exercise of recognizing instances when the Spirit prompts them or the Lord blesses them and discussing them together every evening during dinner. Choose a specific principle you would like to focus on, and discuss it regularly during family meals. Encourage your children to look for examples of courage, virtue, gratitude, or another value of choice in their daily lives. Regular discussion at a time when you are all together can raise your children's awareness of a concept and teach them its value.

President Ezra Taft Benson remembered his mother often singing "Have I Done Any Good in the World Today?"[8] while she worked around the home. Elder Neal A. Maxwell of the Quorum of the Twelve Apostles grew up in a home where the gospel was constantly discussed around the dinner table or while the family worked together.[9] President Gordon B. Hinckley's grandson James Pearce recalled his grandmother's conversations as being peppered with small statements of faith and testimony such as, "Wouldn't life be terrible without the gospel?" and "The gospel's true. I'm sure you know that as well as I do."[10] Such consistent messages of faith from parents may teach children to think and recognize how the gospel affects them in daily life.

Other times, significant life events grant parents special teaching moments. When President Joseph F. Smith was a small boy, his family fled threatening mobs in Nauvoo and camped under trees on the other side of the Mississippi River. He remembers his widowed mother repeatedly telling her children that "the Lord [would] open the way," and her faith inspired her son. Despite the distant sound of cannons and the lack of comforts and conveniences, he remembered feeling "just as certain in [his] mind then—as certain as a child could feel—that all was right, that the Lord's hand was in it."[11]

Similarly President Harold B. Lee's daughter Helen recalled an experience when her father used life's events to instruct his children. On a hike up to a cave her mother had warned her to hold her father's hand and not get too close to the edge of the trail. As they hiked President Lee told his daughters that at times in life he wouldn't be there to protect them from life's cliffs. At

8 Leonard J. Arrington, Susan Arrington Madsen, Emily Madsen Jones, *Mothers of the Prophets* (2009), 221.

9 Bruce C. Hafen, *A Disciple's Life: The Biography of Neal A. Maxwell* (2002), 66.

10 *Glimpses into the Life and Heart of Marjorie Pay Hinckley,* ed. Virginia H. Pearce (1999), 19–20.

11 *Teachings of Presidents of the Church: Joseph F. Smith* (1998), xiv.

these times, they could know that their Heavenly Father was watching and protecting them, and they could always call on the Lord for help. "That lesson has never been forgotten and my understanding of my relationship with my Heavenly Father began in that early childhood experience," Helen said.[12]

Frequent gospel conversations teach children about gospel topics, help them understand how those principles apply in daily life, and give children a setting for asking questions. Notice your children's receptivity as you naturally share your faith and testimony. Observing these reactions and responding with the Spirit can help a parent answer questions children might not be asking vocally and give clues about their faith and testimony.

Family Testimony Meetings

In addition to spontaneous gospel sharing, parents might plan occasional structured times to share testimony. President M. Russell Ballard recommended parents "consider holding a family testimony meeting where parents and children can express their beliefs and feelings to each other in a private and personal setting."[13] On one occasion Elder Neal A. Maxwell took each of his children aside so he could privately bear his testimony to them. (What a precious opportunity for parents to see how their child responds to a testimony of gospel truths!) One daughter recalled that this experience was deeply meaningful and showed how important the gospel was to her father.[14] A generation later Elder Maxwell instituted "Grandpa Neal's firesides" with his grandchildren, where he would share testimony and truths.[15]

When our children were young, we introduced a tradition of family testimony meetings. On fast Sunday we would encourage the children to build a little pulpit in our living room by propping a file box on top of the piano bench and setting up a kitchen utensil as a microphone. Each family member would then take turns at the pulpit sharing their testimony. This tradition has provided a simple opportunity for us to teach our children while they were small the elements of an appropriate testimony. It also gives Cameron and me a personal setting to share things that are important. We like to keep these meetings short, sweet, and light. Of course, no one is compelled to share, and if people really want to stay in their seats rather than go to the pulpit, that's okay. The important thing is the opportunity to practice sharing faith we hold dear.

---

12 L. Brent Goates, *Harold B. Lee: Prophet and Seer* (1985), 117–18.

13 M. Russell Ballard, "What Matters Most Is What Lasts Longest," *Ensign*, Nov. 2005, 43.

14 Hafen, *A Disciple's Life*, 232.

15 Hafen, *A Disciple's Life*, 236–37.

How might family testimony meetings—in whatever form is comfortable for your family—teach faith and strengthen family members?

Following the Prophet

Another important way for parents to convey faith to their children is through following the prophet and apostles. We cannot afford to be carefree in our attitudes toward the prophets and their counsel. Sometimes heeding prophetic words is not popular and can become a source of contention or ridicule. Yet in the days leading up to the Second Coming of Christ, our only true safety is in following the prophet and teaching our children to do the same.

Parents can make simple choices to share testimony of living prophets. One of the easiest is to pray for the prophet and apostles in family prayer and to encourage children to do the same. Our prophets have often asked members to pray for them and other leaders.[16] Praying for our leaders demonstrates faith and helps children build their faith in Church leadership. Parents can also share testimony during daily life and conversation. Talk to your children about the recent counsel from the prophet, or share how following the prophet throughout your life has blessed you. President James E. Faust remembered listening to his grandmother, who had known every prophet from Brigham Young through Heber J. Grant, testify that when people turn their backs on the prophet, they don't prosper. "We were taught the lesson that we should always be found sustaining the leadership of the Church," he said.[17]

Testimony of the prophets—and determination to follow them—is also conveyed through artwork. Elder William R. Walker of the Seventy remembered his grandparents having a framed photo of the First Presidency of the Church in the entryway of their home. As a boy he would look at the photo and think about why his grandparents displayed it prominently in their home. He recognized it as a symbol of their faith and devotion, and that had a powerful influence on him.[18] In our home we decided to hang a picture of the First Presidency by our TV as a visual reminder that the media our family chooses should be in line with the gospel principles taught by Church leaders.

In addition to sharing snippets of testimony and silently conveying faith through artwork, it is imperative for parents to share faith through their life's choices. Elder Bruce R. McConkie's children witnessed their father's determination to follow prophetic counsel when President Spencer W. Kimball

---

16 Thomas S. Monson, "Until We Meet Again," *Ensign*, Nov. 2011, 109.

17 James P. Bell, *In the Strength of the Lord: The Life and Teachings of James E. Faust* (1999), 22.

18 William R. Walker, "Three Presiding High Priests," *Ensign*, May 2008, 37.

encouraged the Saints to grow gardens. The McConkies' yard did not provide a natural spot for a garden, so Elder McConkie decided to reconfigure the yard to make room. "This meant tearing out a beautiful old hedge at the cost of some scratches and sore muscles. It meant the loss of a wonderful little shady spot and also any privacy in the backyard."[19] But it meant that the McConkies followed the prophet, and that was their clear priority.

Another beautiful example of determination to follow the prophet at any cost was displayed in the lives of Andrew and Olive Kimball, parents of President Spencer W. Kimball. Settled comfortably in Salt Lake City, within walking distance of family members, they had six small children and a house payment when Andrew was called to move his family to Arizona and serve as president of the St. Joseph Stake. At that time Arizona was considered a barren wasteland, inhospitable to civilization, and accepting a call to move there required incredible sacrifice. Andrew and Olive "bowed before God trying to pray while their hearts were so swollen with grief. They bubbled over with scalding tears and after a long and hard struggle a petition was made to the throne of Grace while a flood of tears gushed forth. This over, nothing remained but to go to work." They packed up their young family and did as President Wilford Woodruff had asked.[20] Later in life their son Spencer chose to live his life with the same level of faith and devotion he had seen in his parents.

General Conference Traditions

We do not always have to move our families to distant, inhospitable climates as did the Kimball family to follow the prophet, but conspicuously listening to and following the prophets sets an unmistakable example for our children. An important place to start is with general conference. Teach your children that listening to general conference is a treasured and anticipated privilege. Build fun family traditions, and use the weeks leading up to conference to prepare your family spiritually.

When our children were small, I made a conference memory game we would often play during family home evening in the weeks leading up to conference. The cards simply had pictures of the First Presidency and Apostles with their names, but it made the names and faces familiar to young minds. If your children are a little older, use dinnertime or other occasions to share

---

19 Joseph Fielding McConkie, *The Bruce R. McConkie Story: Reflections of a Son* (2003), 260–61.

20 Leonard J. Arrington, Susan Arrington Madsen, Emily Madsen Jones, *Mothers of the Prophets* (2009), 189–90.

stories from the lives of the Apostles to teach them a bit more about these leaders. You could even design a guessing game to make the learning enjoyable. Church websites and magazines contain delightful stories to share about our beloved leaders. Review talks and highlights from the previous conference in the weeks leading up to the next one. Encourage family members to pray to be spiritually ready to hear the messages of conference.

When conference arrives, work to create an enjoyable atmosphere. Many families have traditional conference foods and activities. In our family, conference is celebrated with copious amounts of "conference corn," a salty-sweet popcorn mix we only make for conference. (The recipe is included at the end of the chapter.) Every time a child takes notes about a talk, draws a picture of a talk's topic, or earns a conference bingo they can go to the treat table. The treat table is loaded down with goodies everyone has agreed on during family council the previous week—special favorites such as pizza bread, cinnamon rolls, Brazilian cheese rolls, cinnamon chips with fruit salsa, veggie or fruit platters with yummy dips, fruit or Jell-O salads, baked sweet potato fries, cheese sticks, or polenta fries. The Church website has bingo games and coloring books that can be printed to keep young children occupied. The food and anticipation create a festive atmosphere, and everyone looks forward to conference.

One family I know plays a sort of auditory bingo for conference. The mom sets out a bunch of bowls of different kinds of candy or treats, and each bowl has a different key word attached to it. The more coveted kinds of treats are assigned words that are a little bit harder to catch. Each time one of the kids hears a word, they get the corresponding treat.

Many families also have specific traditions for the priesthood or women's sessions of conference. Some dads and sons go out for ice cream or burgers after the priesthood session. President Russell M. Nelson shared that his family's tradition was for the girls to gather and make doughnuts together.[21] When the men in the family returned home from the session, everyone would gather together to eat the doughnuts and listen to the men's recap of the session.

After conference is over, gather your family together for a special family home evening. Discuss conference highlights, and set goals together—both individually and as a family. In the weeks that follow you might watch a conference talk together every Sunday as a family or review conference talks for family night lessons. Once a month or so, on fast Sunday or another workable time, discuss your family's progress on any conference goals you

---

21 Russell M. Nelson, "Our Sacred Duty to Honor Women," *Ensign*, May 1999, 38.

have set. Work to keep the prophet's counsel alive in the hearts of your family members.

Baptism and the Sacrament

Baptism is the first covenant a child makes, and it is an exciting milestone for both child and parents. Before full-time missionaries baptize a new convert they teach a series of lessons and probe for gospel understanding and testimony. Similarly there is much that parents can do to prepare their young converts for baptism.

Different families choose different methods to help their children prepare for the covenant of baptism. Some families help their children memorize the Articles of Faith and have family night lessons on each article and the doctrine it teaches. Many families set aside a family night or two for specific pre-baptism lessons. In our family we identified foundational doctrines we wanted to make sure our children understood before baptism, and in the year leading up to the baptism of each child we dedicated one family home evening lesson each month to these topics. Our topics included the following: our identity as children of God, the council in heaven, the plan of salvation, Christ's role as our Savior, faith, repentance, baptism, the gift of the Holy Ghost, the Apostasy and Restoration, covenants, the sacrament, the importance of obedience and enduring to the end, and fasting and fast offerings.

Shortly before or after your child's baptism, identify the feelings of the Holy Ghost. Helping a child recognize and label the good feeling they experience at their baptism helps them understand that the Lord approves of their choice and that they can keep that good feeling when they follow His commandments. In the weeks leading up to each child's baptism in our family, my husband and I pray consistently together as a couple that our child will feel and recognize the Spirit on their baptism day and understand its significance. Additionally you can encourage your child to pray to be able to feel and recognize the Spirit on their special day.

As your children grow older, continue to emphasize the importance of their baptismal covenants. At appropriate times during scripture study, family night, or other discussions, revisit scriptural examples of covenants. Talk to your children about what they are doing to keep their baptismal covenants. For instance, if we have just finished a family service project, I will remind my children that serving others is one meaningful way they honor their covenants. Studying their scriptures, praying, going to church, and doing family history and temple work are additional ways children keep their covenants.

Teach your children the importance of the sacrament in renewing their covenants. Sunday morning before church I try to remind our children to take a few minutes for an extra prayer to review their week and pray for the Savior's grace to cleanse and strengthen them for the coming week. I will often encourage my young children to be reverent and watch the priests' preparations when the sacrament is being prepared. While it is being passed, I will whisper that the sacrament is a good time to think about Jesus and picture ourselves following Him. When the bread comes around, I whisper that the bread reminds us that because of Christ, we can be resurrected. The water reminds us we can repent and be made clean. Teaching children to appropriately prepare for the sacrament and continually linking the sacrament to their baptismal covenants will remind children of the importance of that first essential gospel ordinance.

Attending the Temple

Another wonderful way for parents to convey faith is through a love of temple attendance. All faithful Latter-day Saint parents dream of their children having happy temple marriages. Start while your children are young to help them share that same vision. Hang a temple picture in your home, and use it as a means to bear testimony. Show your children through your words and actions that the temple is the Lord's house, a place of refuge through the storms of life. Teach your children why you love going to the temple. Testify of the Spirit you feel there and the longing you feel to go there with them one day.

President Ezra Taft Benson recalled a time when his mother set aside her chores to bear her testimony of temple work to him. He saw her ironing white cloth and asked what she was doing. She responded, "These are temple robes, my son. Your father and I are going to the temple." Then she set aside her ironing, sat down with him, and taught him about the importance of temple work and her hopes that her children, grandchildren, and great-grandchildren would grow to love the temple.[22] What an inspiring example of a mother who was in tune, recognized a teaching opportunity, and bore testimony!

Another important tool to steer children toward the temple is family history work. In the previous chapter I suggested activities that can help your children connect with past generations through relating stories and showing pictures. You can set up ancestors as heroes and role models as you discuss values, principles, and successes. For instance, if you are teaching your children the importance of faith or integrity, share a story from the life of an ancestor who demonstrated that virtue. As children grow older, go online with them

22 *Teachings of Presidents of the Church: Ezra Taft Benson* (2014), 167.

and teach them to index. As they approach their twelfth birthday, help them find ancestors whose names they can take to the temple and for whom they can complete gospel ordinances. Attend the temple with your teens occasionally. Make these trips special, memorable, and full of love. Take a minute afterward to talk about how they felt and to share your testimony of temple work.

As children grow, help them learn to look to the temple as a refuge when life seems difficult. Offer to attend the temple with them or fast with them. Share moments when temple attendance has brought you peace. When Ardeth Kapp, former Young Women general president, was growing up, she doubted her intelligence and abilities. On one occasion her parents went on a walk with her around the temple grounds in Cardston, Alberta, where she grew up. They used that environment as an opportunity to teach her to focus on making good choices. If she did, one day she would be able to go inside the temple. "There she would learn all she needed to know to return to her Heavenly Father. . . Although it might be possible to get a degree from one or more universities of the world, if she were to miss the temple, she would miss the highest degree of the celestial kingdom."[23]

How might pointing your teens toward the temple strengthen and sustain them through their challenges?

Attend the temple as frequently as your circumstances allow, and let your children feel your love of temple service. One of the first things Cameron mentioned to me after we decided to get married was the importance of temple attendance. He remembered his parents attending the temple together every Thursday for much of his youth, and he wanted us to attend the temple together as frequently as possible. I was impressed by the silent example of my in-laws. Regularly attending the temple together while raising a family requires sacrifice. I am sure sometimes it wasn't easy. Perhaps they never dreamed what their choices were teaching, but their temple attendance made an impression and set a standard for my husband to follow.

Missions

In addition to teaching your children to look to the temple, consider ways you can help them look forward to missionary service. Some of these opportunities are basic and easy to adopt. Regularly pray for the missionaries in family prayer, and teach your children to do the same. It is a simple habit, but it raises children's awareness of missionaries. President Spencer W. Kimball counseled, "If [a child] sees his parents going to the temple frequently, he will

23 Anita Thompson, *Stand As a Witness: The Biography of Ardeth Greene Kapp* (2005), 59.

begin to plan a temple life. If he is taught to pray for the missionaries, he will gradually gravitate toward the missionary program. Now, this is very simple, but it is the way of life."[24] If a friend, neighbor, or family member is serving a mission, occasionally sit down together as a family on a Sunday evening or during family night to write the missionary an email or letter. You might even send a small package for a special occasion. Helping children write letters, shop for small items, or bake cookies for a missionary they know may plant a seed of love for missionaries and other service.

The annals of Church history are filled with beautiful stories of sacrifice as children learned to love missionary service from watching their parents' examples. One story is from the early life of President Ezra Taft Benson. His father received a mission call when his mother was expecting their eighth child. Together his parents shed tears and told their children, "We're so proud that Father's considered worthy to go on a mission. We're crying a little because it means two years of separation, and your father and I have never been separated more than two nights at a time since our marriage."[25] Their family sold eighty acres and shared their home with a young couple to help with their crops while their father was gone.[26] Whenever a letter would come from their father, their mother would gather the children and read the missionary experiences aloud. Through the years of sacrifice, something tangible was obviously taught: all eleven Benson children served missions at some point in their lives.

Missionary service is different in our day, but you can still share the missionary spirit with your children in meaningful ways. If your children are young, tell them mission stories for an occasional bedtime story. Include stories from your own mission or that of a spouse, family member, or someone from Church history. Consider writing down significant mission stories and including pictures to make them enjoyable for your children to read. Missions are hard work, but they also provide incomparable growth and joy. Help your children catch the joy of missionary service through stories, experiences, or letters from missionaries they know. Teach them that a mission is something worth sacrificing and preparing for.

In the October 2011 priesthood session of general conference, Elder Jeffrey R. Holland of the Quorum of the Twelve Apostles gave a powerful talk about missionary service. Speaking to older couples, he emphasized that as grandparents serve missions they teach "by deed as well as word, 'In this family

---

24 *Teachings of Presidents of the Church: Spencer W. Kimball* (2006), 207.
25 Sheri L. Dew, *Ezra Taft Benson: A Biography* (Salt Lake City: Deseret Book, 1987), 30.
26 Dew, *Ezra Taft Benson*, 30.

we serve missions!'"[27] I was struck by that thought the first time I read Elder Holland's talk. My mission was a challenging, joyful, formative experience for me, and I longed for a way to teach my children that "in [our] family we serve missions." I began to compile a book of "Mom's Mission Stories," complete with pictures and stories—some fun, some humorous, and some spiritual and meaningful. Cameron and I compiled some of his mission stories, and we have added stories from a few other ancestors. My children tend to naturally gravitate toward the funny stories about the mice in my little trailer home or the goofy tracting songs I made up to sing on long country roads when houses were few and far between. But in the process they learn to look toward missions as times of joy and growth.

You can take additional steps to help a teen prepare for missionary service. Actively encourage as much seminary and institute participation as you can. Work together as a family to memorize scriptures that would help a youth on a mission. Post them by your kitchen table, recite them together at breakfast or dinner, and discuss their meaning and significance. When possible, encourage your youth to go to teaching appointments with the full-time missionaries. The example of faithful, devoted missionaries (and returned missionaries) can be motivating and inspiring. Obtain a copy of *Preach My Gospel*, study it as a family or one-on-one with your teen, and use some of the lessons for family home evenings.

Finally, teach your children to look toward missionary service by helping them save money. Elder L. Tom Perry encouraged prospective missionaries to "set a goal to earn enough money from your part- or full-time work to pay for at least a significant part of your mission" and promised "great blessings— social, physical, mental, emotional, and spiritual blessings—to every young man who pays for a significant part of his mission."[28] When children are young, help them start saving money. Talk to them about the mission they will serve and help them feel anticipation. Some families offer a matching program, matching a certain amount or percentage for each bit their child saves. Others deposit money in their children's mission savings accounts for each scripture they memorize. As your children grow, make sure they are actively aware of anything you do to save money for their future missions. Help them feel aware and invested as you both anticipate their missionary service.

Priesthood Power

Priesthood power is a unique aspect of the restored Church. Without the priesthood, we wouldn't have baptism, the gift of the Holy Ghost, the

---

27 Jeffrey R. Holland, "We Are All Enlisted," *Ensign*, Nov. 2011, 46.
28 L. Tom Perry, "Raising the Bar," *Ensign*, Nov. 2007, 49.

sacrament, the temple and its ordinances and covenants, or a prophet to lead our Church. Not only do we claim power directly from our Savior Jesus Christ to both minister and administer but we also actively ordain youth and teach them to go forth and serve and bless others in the Savior's name. Priesthood power is sacred, and there is much parents can do to prepare their children to honor and respect this holy privilege.

As with other aspects of teaching children faith, one of the basic things parents can do is set an example. Develop a home environment in which priesthood blessings are cherished. Teach children the priesthood is God's power delegated to men. Let them quietly listen when another family member receives a blessing. Set an example of requesting priesthood blessings during times of struggle. Consider keeping personal notes from priesthood blessings. Writing down counsel and promises from priesthood blessings can provide strength and hope. Writing down the things your child is told in priesthood blessings provides you wonderful insights into who your child is in God's eyes and enables you to remind your child of that vision in quiet, sacred moments. Keeping notes from priesthood blessings also sets a powerful example for children and shows them that priesthood blessings are from God and should be cherished and heeded.

Many families develop a tradition of giving children father's blessings at the beginning of a school year, and this is a natural way to teach children to respect the priesthood. At these times parents can explain to children the sacred nature of the priesthood and that a spirit of preparation, peace, and reverence makes it easier for the priesthood holder to hear the quiet whisperings of the Spirit.

Witnessing the faith of a parent and the power of the priesthood provides children a foundation for building a testimony of the Restoration. When President Joseph F. Smith was a small boy, his widowed mother worked hard to help her family cross the plains to the Salt Lake Valley. At one point one of her best oxen seemed to be at the point of death. Mary Fielding Smith went to her wagon to retrieve her consecrated oil, took it to her brother Joseph, and asked him to administer to her ox. After receiving the blessing, the ox stood up and kept going as if nothing had happened. Later another ox had the same problem, Mary chose the same solution, and the ox was healed.[29] What an important lesson this mother's faith taught her children about the power of the priesthood!

Elder Neal A. Maxwell was similarly affected by witnessing the power of the priesthood in his home as a teen. Returning home late from work one night he found his parents and others gathered around the dining room table.

---

29 Leonard J. Arrington, Susan Arrington Madsen, Emily Madsen Jones, *Mothers of the Prophets* (2009), 105.

On the table lay his six-week-old sister, who had whooping cough and seemed to have stopped breathing. Neal watched as his father and the other men administered to the baby and pronounced a blessing of healing. Immediately the baby began to breathe, and Neal's mother bundled her up and rushed her to the hospital. Neal went to his room and knelt to pray and thank the Lord for his parents' faith.[30]

Preparing Sons to Honor Their Priesthood

In addition to setting an example of faith in the power of the priesthood, take steps to actively prepare your sons to hold and honor the priesthood. As a son approaches each age of priesthood advancement (twelve, fourteen, sixteen, and eighteen), sit down together for one-on-one time to talk. Read significant scriptural passages about the priesthood together. Doctrine and Covenants sections 20, 84, and 107 are a good place to start, and Alma 13 also teaches beautiful doctrine about the priesthood. Review what the priesthood is, what office your son will be receiving, and what his responsibilities and blessings will be. Memorize the sacrament prayers together. Answer questions and probe for insights into his feelings and testimony. Share your testimony about how the priesthood blesses your life. Throughout your son's Aaronic Priesthood years sit down with him occasionally, as he is willing, to read a general conference priesthood session talk. You can compile a list of favorite talks with key points you would like to teach or print and collect them into a binder. Discuss ideas and teach your son the incredible power the Lord has entrusted him with. Teach your son that holding the priesthood is a sacred opportunity to serve as Christ would serve.

Elder Jeffrey R. Holland's son Matthew shared how his dad had helped him prepare for priesthood service in a simple way. "I . . . remember my father telling me a few weeks before I was ordained a deacon that he hoped whenever I prepared, blessed, or passed the sacrament I would always wear a white shirt and a tie. I'm sure I had heard the same advice from a Sunday School teacher or had read it in some manual, but it wasn't until my father said it that I intended to do it. . . . And that small word of advice also helped me understand that priesthood ordinances are not just work or assignments, but they are priceless privileges that I'm grateful to take part in."[31] Parents who actively participate in teaching doctrine and preparing their sons for priesthood service teach powerful lessons and prepare their children for beautiful experiences.

30 Bruce C. Hafen, *A Disciple's Life: The Biography of Neal A. Maxwell* (2002), 67–68.
31 Matthew S. Holland, "Muddy Feet and White Shirts," *Ensign*, May 1983, 39.

Tithing

In addition to preparing children for temple worthiness, missionary service, and honoring the priesthood, it is wise for parents to prepare children to be faithful tithe payers. Tithing is a principle of faith. We don't pay tithing because we feel we have money to spare; we pay tithing because it's a commandment and we have faith in God and His promises. Children can be prepared to observe this law through observing their parents' faith and hearing their testimonies.

As with other aspects of gospel observance, seeds of faith are first planted through the parents' example. Openly share your experiences and testimony with your children during family home evening lessons or other appropriate times.

President Joseph F. Smith was instructed by the example of his widowed mother, who insisted on paying tithing, no matter how destitute her circumstances. On one occasion when she took her tithing to the tithing office, one of the receiving clerks told her she wasn't wise to pay tithing and that tithing should be paid by those who were more financially sturdy. Mary Fielding Smith responded, "Would you deny me a blessing? If I did not pay my tithing, I should expect the Lord to withhold his blessings from me. I pay my tithing, not only because it is a law of God, but because I expect a blessing by doing it." President Smith concluded, "She prospered because she obeyed the laws of God."[32]

President James E. Faust observed similar faithfulness—and made similar conclusions—about his grandfather. During the Depression his grandfather was behind on the taxes owed on his farm, and a drought was killing his cattle. Yet when it was time to harvest the hay, his grandfather instructed them to go to the corner of the field where the best hay was and harvest that for tithing. Young Jim wondered how his grandfather and his farm would survive and marveled at his grandfather's faith. He recalled, "The legacy of faith he passed on to his posterity was far greater than money, because he established in the minds of his children and grandchildren that above all he loved the Lord and His holy work over other earthly things. He never became wealthy, but he died at peace with the Lord and with himself."[33]

Elder David A. Bednar's wife, Susan, was taught the blessings of tithing by a faithful mother. At one point in her youth, Susan's mother was reviewing their family's financial expenses and noted that their family had fewer medical

32 *Teachings of Presidents of the Church: Joseph F. Smith* (1998), 49.
33 James P. Bell, *In the Strength of the Lord: The Life and Teachings of James E. Faust* (1999), 33.

expenses than might have been expected. She attributed this blessing to their payment of tithes.[34] Tithing provides an opportunity for parents to teach children about the blessings they receive financially, physically, or spiritually. When faith is exercised and tithing is paid, faith continues to grow as the Lord's invitation is tested and proven in individual lives. Sometimes tithing doesn't result in financial prosperity and the best blessings from the payment of tithes are spiritual. Other times we may discern hidden blessings aside from financial or spiritual ones. Teaching children to notice subtle blessings from paying tithing can strengthen their testimony and bolster their faith.

When children are young, begin to teach them to pay tithing and fast offerings. President Spencer W. Kimball recalled his father's gentle way of helping his children pay their tithing. Young Spencer and his sister were each given a patch of potatoes to care for. After harvesting, cleaning, and selling the potatoes, the children returned home jubilant. Their father asked what they planned to do with their newfound wealth, and the children immediately started listing off their ideas—candy, ice cream, and Christmas presents. "Now, you haven't forgotten the bishop have you?" queried their father. "The Lord has been kind to us. We planted and cultivated and harvested, but the earth is the Lord's. He sent the moisture and the sunshine. One-tenth we always give back to the Lord for his part." President Kimball recalled that his father didn't make demands but gently taught the doctrine "so convincingly that we felt it an honor and privilege to pay tithing."[35]

Many parents begin to introduce the concept of tithing when their children are small. Young children naturally want to do what's right, and tithing isn't a difficult concept for them. I love the way President Kimball's father couched it: they did some work, but the Lord blessed them with increase. Instilling the why of tithing in young children is important and helps them to grow up feeling gratitude rather than entitlement.

Additionally, when children turn eight, they may be ready to observe the principle of the fast—perhaps for just a few hours in the beginning. At this time parents might also encourage their children to pay a small fast offering. Again, the principle of the fast is a principle of faith and shows our desire to draw closer to God. Teach your children that the Lord is generous with us and that we should be generous with others. As we reach out to bless the lives of those around us—through fast offerings and other means—we know the Lord will care for us in our times of need. When we care for others, the Savior views

---

34 David A. Bednar, "The Windows of Heaven," *Ensign*, Nov. 2013, 17.
35 Edward L. Kimball and Andrew E. Kimball Jr., *Spencer W. Kimball: Twelfth President of the Church of Jesus Christ of Latter-day Saints* (1977), 32.

it as if we were reaching out to care for Him. These are powerful principles to instill in children from their youth.

There is much parents can do in their homes, quietly and simply, to plant faith in their children. All of these small actions boil down to a love of our Father in Heaven, our Savior, and Their gospel. The more we cultivate faith in our homes, the more we demonstrate our love of the Lord for our children and teach them to love Him too. Margaret D. Nadauld observed, "Then surely we must help our children love Him. . . . It is just that simple. We must help them love Him, feel tender toward Him, be grateful for Him, know Him, honor Him, serve Him."[36] That love—springing from the Holy Ghost and filling us with love of Jesus Christ, our Heavenly Father, and others—is the soul of conversion and joy. In our homes we can consistently work to build faith and love in our children one conversation, one family home evening lesson, and one testimony at a time.

Application

1. Walk around your home and consider your artwork. What message does it convey? Consider additional messages you might want to emphasize.
2. Consider specific values you would like to emphasize. Encourage family members to look for ways these values affect their daily lives. Discuss them every night at dinner.
3. Hold a family testimony meeting for your family to enjoy on occasion.
4. What counsel has the prophet given recently? Consider how your family might follow the counsel more fully.
5. Seek ways to implement conference traditions that will help your family rejoice in and follow prophetic counsel a little better.
6. If your child hasn't been baptized yet, consider ways to meaningfully prepare him for baptism and the gift of the Holy Ghost.
7. On Sunday mornings remind children to pray and prepare to meaningfully partake of the sacrament.
8. Show your children temple pictures. (Pictures from inside newly built temples are sometimes available on mormonnewsroom.org.) Bear your testimony of temple work.
9. If you have teenagers, schedule regular times to go to the temple together. Make these special occasions, with an outpouring of love.
10. Go to the temple as much as your circumstances allow.

---

36 Margaret D. Nadauld, *A Mother's Influence: Raising Children to Change the World* (2004), 20.

11. Compile mission stories and pictures from relatives' missions for your children to read.
12. Occasionally write to missionaries your family knows.
13. Memorize mission preparation scriptures as a family.
14. Occasionally use *Preach My Gospel* lessons for family home evening.
15. Help your children save money for their missions.
16. Write down promises and counsel from priesthood blessings in your personal journal. Occasionally reflect on these promises to give you strength and hope.
17. Help priesthood-aged sons prepare for each priesthood ordination through one-on-one study sessions.
18. Teach your children the law of the fast, and help them pay fast offerings.

Sullivan Family Conference Corn Recipe

Combine one (very) large bowl of popcorn with a large bag of Fritos corn chips and a half a box of Corn Pops cereal. Melt 8 ounces of white chocolate, drizzle it over the mixture, and stir well.

CHAPTER 3
Prayer

I know of no other practice that will have so salutary an effect upon your lives as will the practice of kneeling together in prayer. —Gordon B. Hinckley[1]

PRAYER IS A PRINCIPLE WITH great potential for families. Prayers can be thoughtless, repetitive, and perfunctory, or prayers can be a sublime form of communication with God. The Bible Dictionary states, "As soon as we learn the true relationship in which we stand toward God (namely, God is our Father, and we are His children), then at once prayer becomes natural and instinctive on our part" (Bible Dictionary, "Prayer"). We have a tremendous responsibility as parents to teach our children who they are and how to talk to their Eternal Father. The things we directly and indirectly teach them about prayer can impact them throughout their lives.

President Heber J. Grant remembered his mother's prayers as being powerful and motivational. "So near to the Lord would she get in her prayers that they were a wonderful inspiration to me from childhood to manhood."[2] How can parents improve their own prayers? How can family prayer be managed to strengthen the family unit?

It is easy to get into a prayer rut and recite a typical list of things we want. President Harold B. Lee taught, "There is a lot of difference between saying a prayer and talking with God. Do not say prayers, do not read prayers, but learn to talk with God."[3] How can parents teach their children to truly talk with God?

Let's explore some ways prayer can revitalize your family as a whole.

---

1 Gordon B. Hinckley, *Cornerstones of a Happy Home* (pamphlet, 1984), 10.
2 Leonard J. Arrington, Susan Arrington Madsen, Emily Madsen Jones, *Mothers of the Prophets* (2009), 110.
3 *Teachings of Presidents of the Church: Harold B. Lee* (2000), 52.

Building Your Personal Prayer Relationship with God
The Power of a Parent's Prayers

Have you ever wondered what your personal prayer habits teach your children? Have your children ever walked in on you praying? Do they know how your prayers have been answered? Do they see your faith and prayers blessing your family?

Parents who pray consistently, sincerely, and intently bless their families with their faith. Sometimes parents feel tired, hurried, and distracted, and taking a few extra minutes for meaningful prayer can fall to the bottom of their priority list. While we know prayer is important, it is easy to lose sight of the incredible power of prayer in the daily life of a parent. Let's consider some ways praying with your whole heart and soul can impact your family.

On the night Joseph Smith went to Hill Cumorah to get the gold plates, his mother, Lucy Mack Smith, "spent the night in prayer and supplication to God."[4] How much strength was granted to Joseph simply because of his mother's faith and prayers? How might your prayers for your children strengthen them to fulfill their missions in life?

When Elder Neal A. Maxwell served in World War II, he was involved in a critical battle at Okinawa. At one point, worried that he was being targeted by enemy fire, he pleaded with the Lord to spare his life. Suddenly the firing ceased. Decades later he learned that during that time period his parents had knelt together to pray one night as they did every night. As they got into bed his mother had told his father, "We must get up and pray again. Neal is in grave danger."[5] How many people both in the Church and out were affected by this miracle wrought by his parents' faith? How might your prayers for your child's safety make a difference, perhaps in ways you might never know in this life?

When President Heber J. Grant's first wife was dying, he called their children in to say goodbye to their mother. His twelve-year-old daughter begged him to administer to her mother so she wouldn't die. President Grant told his daughter that everyone has a time appointed for them to die, and he felt assured it was his wife's time to return home. After the children left the room President Grant knelt and pleaded for the Lord to let his daughter know it was her mother's time to die. Shortly thereafter his wife died, their children came back into the room, and one young son started crying. The twelve-year-old daughter comforted her brother and said, "Since we went out of this room the voice of the Lord from heaven has said to me, 'In the death

4 Lucy Mack Smith, *History of Joseph Smith,* ed. Preston Nibley (1958), 102, as cited in *Teachings of Presidents of the Church: Harold B. Lee* (2000), 141.
5 Bruce C. Hafen, *A Disciple's Life: The Biography of Neal A. Maxwell* (2002), 115.

of your mamma the will of the Lord shall be done.'"[6] She was bolstered and blessed through an extreme trial by her father's faith and prayers. How might your prayers for your children's comfort, strength, peace, and understanding uphold them in the trials the Lord gives them?

Once during President Harold B. Lee's teenage years, his mother came to him "with an intuitive impression and warning," which he brushed off. Within the month he found himself facing the very temptation his mother had warned him about. He later counseled parents, "If you ever have sons and daughters who amount to what they should in the world, it will be in no small degree due to the fact that your children have a mother who spends many nights on her knees in prayer, praying God that her son, her daughter, will not fail."[7] How might your prayers and inspiration provide needed buffering in temptations faced by your child?

Toward the end of the Zion's Camp expedition the Prophet Joseph Smith and Hyrum were quite ill with cholera. After praying together for healing, Hyrum exclaimed that he had received a vision in which he saw their mother kneeling and praying under an apple tree, pleading for God to spare her sons' lives. Hyrum told Joseph, "The Spirit testifies, that her prayers, united with ours, will be answered." Joseph responded, "Oh, my mother!" When he returned home, he said, "How often have your prayers been a means of assisting us when the shadows of death encompassed us!"[8] How many blessings is God willing to bestow on us and our children if we simply exercise our faith and call on His hand? How might your faith and prayers bring blessings into your children's lives—blessings God is willing to grant but that hinge on faith and prayer?

No wonder President M. Russell Ballard counseled mothers, "Pray deeply about your children and about your role as a mother."[9] Your prayers can call down miracles and blessings for your family.

The Power of a Parent's Example

In addition to blessing your children with your heavenly petitions, your prayer habits teach your children much about faith and its potential in their lives. Often parents' prayers are their children's first introduction to faith in action, their first witness that God is real.

---

6 *Teachings of Presidents of the Church: Heber J. Grant* (2002), 47–48.
7 *Teachings of Presidents of the Church: Harold B. Lee* (2000), 141.
8 Leonard J. Arrington, Susan Arrington Madsen, Emily Madsen Jones, *Mothers of the Prophets* (2009), 20–21.
9 M. Russell Ballard, "Daughters of God," *Ensign*, May 2008, 110.

When you are firmly grounded in your discipleship, your conversations with God will flow freely and naturally. In that process your prayer habits will become transparent for your children, and they may learn where to turn in their hardships. Such was the case with President Joseph F. Smith, who traveled across the plains as a young boy with his widowed mother and other family members. One morning they awoke to find their best team of oxen missing. After young Joseph and his uncle searched extensively, he returned first to their wagons and happened upon his mother kneeling in prayer, pleading that the lost team could be found. When she stood up from her prayer, she smiled and encouraged her son and brother to enjoy breakfast while she went to look for the oxen. Ignoring one man's suggestion that she look in the opposite direction, she soon found the oxen. President Smith later recalled, "It made an indelible impression upon my mind, and has been a source of comfort, assurance and guidance to me throughout all of my life."[10]

Do your children know of your prayers and the subsequent guidance you receive? In their earliest years can they draw water from your well of faith as they see your prayers raining down blessings on your family?

Once during a major debate tournament in his senior year of high school, President Harold B. Lee and his teammate beat a team no one in their school's history had ever conquered. Feeling pleased about his accomplishment, he called home to share his victory. His mother told him she already knew about it. She later explained, "When I knew it was just time for this performance to start, I went out among the willows by the creekside, and there, all by myself, I remembered you and prayed God you would not fail." Young Harold realized his mother's faith had blessed him and that his victories were due to God's help and his mother's love.[11]

Witnessing your prayers, answers, and guidance authenticates all the other faith habits you instill in your home. Faith first becomes real for children as they see that prayer works, God lives, and He cares for us. When your children see your faith in action, they may instinctively learn to pray during their own struggles. Share your experiences with your family over dinner or at other appropriate moments. Tell your children how the Lord has directed or blessed you. Show your children the deep power of active prayer.

Involving Children in Prayers

While many of a parent's prayers will be alone and in quiet moments, it is also appropriate for parents to involve their children in their prayers. In

10 *Teachings of the Presidents of the Church: Joseph F. Smith* (1998), 21–22.
11 Blaine M. Yorgason, *Humble Servant, Spiritual Giant: The Story of Harold B. Lee* (2001), 50–52.

moments when you have just received news that merits a prayer of gratitude or a plea for strength, when you are driving and need to pray for direction or for safety, or when another family member needs extra prayers, invite your children to join their faith with yours. Allow them to see the Lord as your source of hope and reassurance.

Demonstrating faith in prayer was an area in which President Ezra Taft Benson's wife, Flora, excelled. Her children remembered their mother as a woman of incredible faith. "When mother prayed, you knew her prayers were getting through the roof," recalled one son. "She got very specific with the Lord in her prayers and talked out situations with Him; even as a little boy I felt that when she prayed for me, things would work out fine." He remembered often finding his mother in her room praying over a problem at the very moment a challenging situation had arisen. A daughter recalled, "She believed the Lord was interested in every little thing that was taking place in our lives." And another son said, "At the drop of a hat, she'd be on her knees, praying for her children, whether it was about a test or a fight on the school grounds, it didn't matter."[12]

Sister Benson's prayer habit taught her children many lessons. Through her example they learned to pray for specifics and to talk to the Lord about the details of their lives. They observed her habit of praying at the exact moment someone needed a blessing. They saw her faith drive her to her knees in large and small matters. These observations gave her children faith and comfort— they knew God heard her prayers.

When your children see you pray or join in your prayers, they feel strength and reassurance. They know God is in charge and ready to bless your family. As you pray diligently, specifically, and intentionally, your children may quietly learn faith is real.

Improving Personal Prayers

Life is busy for everyone, and that is especially true for parents. Many young parents are awoken early and throughout the night by children who need help, and the opportunity to pray can seem difficult to find. Prayerfully consider your schedule, needs, and routine. Counsel with the Lord about what you might change to make your prayer habits most effective. At times I have found it helpful to set a goal for a minimum prayer length. For instance, if I have set a goal to pray for at least five minutes in the evening, I won't be tempted to rush through my prayer and climb into bed. I will take the time I need to truly counsel with the Lord, and often my prayers will exceed my goal time, and I will feel more spiritually uplifted. Other times I have found

---

12 Sheri L. Dew, *Ezra Taft Benson: A Biography* (1987), 139.

it more effective to try to pause a couple of extra times throughout the day, rather than just in the morning and evening, to pray. Praying more constantly allows me to share my heart and my day with the Lord in brief, comforting snippets that bring me peace and answers without taking a long chunk of time all at once. Praying vocally, rather than just in my mind and heart, also helps me stay focused and engaged as I talk with the Lord. Seasons of life vary with different demands. Find a habit that works for you now. When it doesn't work anymore, reevaluate and find something better. The more devoted you are to communicating with the Lord, the more your life will be blessed and your children will witness your faith and purity.

Most of us first learn to pray by reciting lists of things we are grateful for and lists of things we want. At some point we all must learn to counsel with the Lord as we pray. Sometimes it is helpful to pause for a moment before you begin praying—gather your thoughts and reflect on your day. You might think of a hymn to help you feel reverent and prepared or contemplate what you need to talk to the Lord about. Consider Joseph Smith's First Vision. When young Joseph was visited by the Father and the Son, it was not in his home where people may have been running about creating distractions. Joseph had determined to find a quiet place to pray vocally (see Joseph Smith—History 1:14–15). Properly prepared to receive revelation, Joseph experienced one of the greatest spiritual manifestations recorded in the scriptures.

What can you do to prepare for meaningful prayer and spiritual impressions?

One method that has helped me prepare for prayer is to keep a prayer notebook. In my notebook I will scratch down thoughts or notes I need to talk to the Lord about, such as a child's persistent behavior problem or a vexing situation I need help with. Throughout the day, when the need arises, I will jot a note down in my prayer notebook. Writing down ideas here and there as they come to me enables me to pray specifically over scenarios in which I need extra guidance. Having a notebook handy during my prayer can also be useful to record inspiration that comes. I can then refer back to those answers in the days or weeks that follow to make sure I don't forget the answers I receive.

I start a fresh page in my prayer notebook each week. I leave space for each family member and anything I might need to pray for about them. I jot down notes and reminders of Christlike attributes I am working on so I can see them and remember to pray for them. I also write down the names of people I minister to or other people or concerns I need to be praying about. Keeping a prayer notebook is one way to show that you are serious about talking with the Lord and receiving inspiration.

While you pray, share your grateful heart with the Lord. Gratitude changes our perspective, helps us feel joy and happiness, and lets us see how actively the Lord blesses and cares for us. Elder David A. Bednar has recommended we occasionally offer prayers of just gratitude.[13] Offering such a prayer sheds pure light on our lives as we recognize how blessed we are, all that God has given us, and how thoroughly He cares for us.

Using Prayer to Help Make Changes

You can use your personal prayers to strengthen you in your parenting and enable you to make Christlike changes. In your morning prayer forecast your day. Talk to the Lord about your schedule and anything that concerns you. Occasionally He might recommend a different plan of action. If you are working on a specific Christlike attribute, such as responding to your children with greater patience, kindness, or cheer, talk to the Lord about it. I have found it helps to envision in my mind different scenarios that might occur throughout the day and to pray about appropriate responses in each situation. Praying about responding to my children in specific, Christlike ways helps me feel more at peace as I start my day and provides an extra boost in moments when I might feel inclined to be less patient or kind.

In your evening prayer, pause and consider anything that happened throughout the day that you need to repent for. Talk to the Lord about what happened and ask how you might handle the situation better in the future. In such moments the Spirit can teach more peaceful, loving ways to deal with those around you. Write down the answers you receive in a prayer notebook, and review them the next day to help you remember how to respond to life's challenges in Christlike ways.

Elder David A. Bednar has instructed that "morning and evening prayers—and all of the prayers in between—are not unrelated, discrete events; rather, they are linked together each day and across days, weeks, months, and even years. This is in part how we fulfill the scriptural admonition to 'pray always.' . . . Such meaningful prayers are instrumental in obtaining the highest blessings God holds in store for His faithful children."[14]

Praying in the morning and envisioning yourself choosing Christlike responses and repenting in the evening and asking the Lord how to manage things better can slowly change your character. Over time such prayers enable the grace of Christ to mold you into a more peaceful, loving disciple of the Lord. Character changes don't happen overnight; they probably won't happen

13 David A. Bednar, "Pray Always," *Ensign*, Nov. 2008, 43.
14 Bednar, "Pray Always," 42.

in a week or even in a month. But as you pray consistently and work diligently over the course of months, your character can be refined through our Savior's grace. He will show you a better way to follow Him, and He will give you the strength to do it. The cost of discipleship is sustained effort; the reward is increased peace and joy.

Family Prayer

In addition to learning about prayer by watching the personal prayer habits of their parents, children are instructed much through the ritual of family prayer. The Savior instructed, "Pray in your families unto the Father, always in my name, that your wives and your children may be blessed" (3 Nephi 18:21).

President Gordon B. Hinckley's wife, Marjorie, explained one reason family prayer is so important. "I think family prayer had a great deal to do with the way our children responded to us," she said. "Even though Gordon didn't preach to them, they heard everything we wanted them to hear in family prayer." One of their sons agreed. "We learned much about the depth of [Dad's] faith by listening to him pray. He addressed God with great reverence . . . and he referred to the Savior with deep feeling. As a child I knew they were real persons to him—that he loved and revered them." President Hinckley regularly prayed for his children, their teachers, the "downtrodden and oppressed," and those who were "alone and afraid." He also prayed that his family would "live without regret."[15] Hearing their father pray sincerely and specifically taught the children that the gospel was true and they had an Eternal Father to turn to in their challenges.

What do the things you pray for in family prayer teach your children? Can your children detect the depth of your faith as you pray deeply, sincerely, and consistently in your family?

When President Heber J. Grant was a boy, he often spent time at President Brigham Young's home and joined in their family prayers. He was similarly affected by President Young's prayers. "Upon more than one occasion . . . I have lifted my head, turned and looked at the place where Brigham Young was praying, to see if the Lord was not there. It seemed to me that he talked to the Lord as one man would talk to another."[16]

Can your children tell you are really speaking with the Lord as you pray and that He is real to you?

15 Sheri L. Dew, *Go Forward with Faith: The Biography of Gordon B. Hinckley* (1996), 171.

16 *Teachings of Presidents of the Church: Heber J. Grant* (2002), 173.

Parents who choose to prioritize family prayer call down blessings for their family and quietly teach their children many things. President Thomas S. Monson has taught that in families who hold family prayer, "Wives will draw closer to their husbands and husbands will all the more appreciate their wives; and children will be happy children."[17] Through their reverence and sincerity such parents teach their children that God is real, that He cares for us, and that He actively blesses us. Parents also demonstrate how dependent we are on God for strength, comfort, love, and blessings. As President Kimball taught, "In our family circles, our children will learn how to talk to their Heavenly Father by listening to their parents. They will soon see how heartfelt and honest our prayers are. If our prayers are hurried, even tending to be thoughtless ritual, they will see this also. Better that we do in our families and in private as Mormon pleaded, 'Wherefore, my beloved brethren, pray unto the Father with all the energy of heart' (Moro. 7:48)."[18] One mother told me that when her family occasionally forgets family prayer and their day begins to unravel, she immediately gathers her children for prayer and explains that their day has been going so poorly because they forgot to pray. What a simple way to teach your children their dependence on God!

Too often our prayers can be, as President Kimball said, hurried and thoughtless. Learning to pray with feeling and depth teaches children that prayer is meaningful and vital. Such prayers also shed light on parental hopes and expectations. President Ezra Taft Benson listened to his mother pray "with all the energy of heart" as a youth, and it affected his behavior. While his father was serving a mission and his mother was home caring for their eight children, his mother would "pray and pray and pray that Father would be successful, that he wouldn't worry about home. She'd pray that our work might go well in the fields, that we'd be kind to each other. . . . When your mother prays with such fervor, night after night, you think twice before you do something to disappoint her."[19]

I love that example of a son who was affected by the sincerity of his mother's prayers. Fervent prayers show our children what is in our hearts, what our hopes are, and where our faith lies. Family prayer provides a way for parents to demonstrate faith, love, and expectations. When family prayer is a firm daily ritual, those expectations, love, and faith can become deeply embedded in the hearts and minds of children.

17 *Teachings of Thomas S. Monson,* comp. Lynne F. Cannegieter (2011), 224.
18 *Teachings of Presidents of the Church: Spencer W. Kimball* (2006), 55.
19 Leonard J. Arrington, Susan Arrington Madsen, Emily Madsen Jones, *Mothers of the Prophets* (2009), 211.

Making Family Prayer Work

There are many ways to adapt family prayer in individual circumstances, as well as a few prophetic guidelines to consider. President Spencer W. Kimball taught, "In the past, having family prayer once a day may have been all right. But in the future it will not be enough if we are going to save our families."[20] If that counsel was true when President Kimball was the prophet, how much more do today's families need to shield their children with prayer? Having family prayer twice a day requires commitment and dedication from the whole family—especially the parents. A little creativity and a sense of humor can help smooth the path.

Morning prayer provides a loving launch pad for children as they start their day. For generations many families held morning prayer just before breakfast. Margaret D. Nadauld recalled that her grandmother would always set the breakfast table the night before with the chairs turned away from the table. Everyone would kneel at their chairs before eating breakfast.[21]

Some families must juggle different schedules and needs for children in different age ranges. Some of these families choose to say family prayers in shifts—praying with kids in groups before they leave for school or other engagements at different times. The how is perhaps less important than just making it happen and spiritually fortifying your family as you start your day.

Consider the needs and feelings of each member when holding family prayer. President Spencer W. Kimball taught, "The family group prayer should be in length and composition appropriate to the need. A prayer of a . . . couple would be different from one for a family of grown children or for one of small children. Certainly, it should not be long when little children are involved, or they may lose interest and tire of prayer and come to dislike it."[22] Pray for your children sincerely. Teach your children to pray for family members and others. But don't make family prayer burdensome.

Holding consistent family prayer is no small task. Sometimes children don't feel like praying, don't want to get out of bed, or generally feel uncooperative. These are times that test parents' mettle—good times to remember the Doctrine and Covenant 121 injunction to choose persuasion, long-suffering, gentleness, meekness, and love. Forcing children to participate will not help them feel the spirit of a prayer, so wise parents will gently remind, ask, and try to persuade. Mary Ellen Smoot, thirteenth Relief Society general president, remembered her father gathering the children for prayer while her mother

20 *Teachings of Presidents of the Church: Spencer W. Kimball* (2006), 55.
21 Margaret D. Nadauld, *A Mother's Influence* (2004), 13.
22 *Teachings of Presidents of the Church: Spencer W. Kimball* (2006), 54.

made breakfast in the mornings. If one of the children wanted to stay in bed, their father would tickle them and say that family prayer couldn't be held without them. She remembered hearing her parents pray for each individual child, along with other family members, missionaries, and Church leaders. She said, "Prayer changes things, and I am a witness that it changes hearts and convinces you there is a Father listening and caring about you as a child because your parents exemplified this principle in their lives."[23] She gained that testimony of prayer in part because of parents who loved and encouraged their children to join family prayer.

Morning prayer is difficult to juggle with family members' varying needs and schedules, but evening prayer can be equally tricky. When children are young and parents have to help with every little detail of bedtime preparation, it is easy to want to rush children off to bed without tacking on one more task of an evening prayer. As children age it is difficult to get everyone together at home at one time for prayer. Do the best you can. Pray for inspiration to know how to best meet everyone's needs. Use gentleness and self-restraint. You are building an eternal family, and the Lord will help you know how to proceed. Some parents use the evening prayer as an opportunity to hug each child before bed, express love, and pay them a sincere compliment on something they did well that day. This can be a wonderful way to send children to bed filled with faith and love.

One single-parent friend whose family has endured a bit of trauma has found strength through a little family prayer ritual. Kneeling together as a family in a circle they hold hands and each family member takes a turn saying a prayer. My friend has found that listening to each child's prayer gives her insights into the heart and concerns of the child. Occasionally after each member has prayed her children will open up about their concerns or heartaches. This particular form of prayer has brought her family comfort and increased unity.

Family prayer requires commitment and constant effort. But it also teaches our children who they are and where they can turn for strength and love.

Teaching Children to Pray

When parents set an example of prayer through developing a personal relationship with God and holding consistent family prayer, they lay a foundation for teaching children how to pray. In the beginning teaching children to pray requires constant tutoring. Toddlers who have grown up observing their family

---

23 Janet Peterson and LaRene Gaunt, *Faith, Hope, and Charity: Inspiration from the Lives of General Relief Society Presidents* (2008), 248.

members pray will understand the basics. When you listen to your children's prayers or teach little ones to pray, encourage them to pause and consider their day. Ask if there are things they are grateful for or concerns they would like to discuss with the Lord. Sometimes parents can offer gentle suggestions. Helping small children develop a habit of daily prayer builds a foundation of faith for the future and gives children a feeling of security.

When parents teach their children to pray, they teach their children who they really are. Teach your children that they are children of God, that they lived with Him before they lived with you, and that He is intimately aware of them and interested in their growth. Such teachings give children a glimpse of what they can become and how important their choices in life are.

What Should Children Pray For?

Parents have a significant opportunity to teach children actively and by example what to pray about. Our children know we like to pray when something is lost, when the traffic is bad or driving weather is inclement, or anytime we're going to be driving for a long distance. If your child has something that worries them, encourage them to pray about it. Praying with a child about their concerns demonstrates love and compassion. When President M. Russell Ballard served as a mission president in Canada, his son had to start kindergarten in a new school where he didn't know anyone. For several days in a row President Ballard knelt with his son in the morning before he went to school and prayed his son would find friends.[24]

When one of our daughters was struggling to develop a character trait that would have aided in her success, I offered to pray with her alone every morning for her individual strength and help. Doing this also allowed me to pray in her presence about how much we love her, how proud we are of her, and how much we trust in the Lord for help. After I prayed she would then pray for help as well. Throughout the day I would actively look for examples of the needed trait developing in her so I could encourage her progress.

Does your child have specific concerns that could be eased if you regularly prayed together with him? Does he need help learning to read, tie his shoes, or master his algebra? How can you join your faith with his and encourage him to pray for help?

What we teach children to pray for can establish traits of humility and selflessness and build unity. Talk to your family about friends, neighbors, or others who could benefit from your faith and prayers. This might be an

---

24 Kathleen Lubeck, "Elder M. Russell Ballard: True to the Faith," *Ensign*, March 1986, 10.

occasional topic during family dinner, or a small list could be posted in a visible place for family members to refer to. Teach your children to pray for the prophet, the missionaries, and people who are sick or burdened. Occasionally a family member will have a specific need, and all family members can be encouraged to remember that person in their daily prayers. Teach your children that when they say the family prayer, they should pray for each individual family member. Praying for others can build compassion and teach children that others need their love and faith. As President Gordon B. Hinckley taught, "In remembering together before the Lord the poor, the needy, and the oppressed, there is developed, unconsciously but realistically, a love for others above self, a respect for others, a desire to serve the needs of others. One cannot ask God to help a neighbor in distress without feeling motivated to do something oneself toward helping that neighbor."[25]

President Ezra Taft Benson's wife, Flora, prayed fervently for the members of her family and taught her children to do the same. One of the Benson daughter's college roommates shared an experience in which she learned about prayer in the Benson family. She attended a session of general conference in the tabernacle with the Benson family. When President David O. McKay announced Elder Benson as the next speaker, she noticed as the six siblings passed a message down the row to each other: "Pray for Dad." At the end of the row she noticed Sister Benson sitting with her head bowed, already silently praying for her husband's success.[26] Sister Benson had demonstrated a personal example of frequent, heartfelt prayer. She had shown her children when to pray and what to pray for. When their father arose to speak in conference, they instinctively knew they should pray for him. What a wonderful example for all parents to emulate!

As children grow older and you no longer listen to their personal prayers it might still be helpful to occasionally inquire about a child's prayer habits. Ask your children if they remember to pray in the morning and evening and if they feel their prayers are answered. Is there anything in your child's life about which he would appreciate your faith and prayers? If your child's habit of morning or evening prayers has lapsed, talk to him about what might help him change. Encourage him to set a goal, and offer any support you can.

Even teenagers can benefit from occasional coaching or inquiry about their prayer habits. Parents have wisdom and experience that can be offered gently in the right time and place. Teen years are often filled with questions as youth decide what they believe and figure out how to follow the Savior. Pray

25 *Teachings of Presidents of the Church: Gordon B. Hinckley* (2016), 111.
26 Elaine S. McKay, "Pray for Dad," *New Era*, June 1975, 33.

for the Spirit's guidance and the right opportunity to talk to your teen about her testimony. Does she feel her prayers are answered? Does she recognize promptings or inspiration from the Spirit? Does she know how to pray to receive answers?

Parents can also lightly point out things for teens to pray for. Teens can learn to pray about big decisions, for strength in trials, and to feel the Lord's love. They can pray for a testimony and the ability to recognize the Spirit. Tad R. Callister, Sunday School general president, recalled a time in his teens when his mother inquired if he was asking the Lord to help him find a good wife. At age seventeen finding a good wife was not one of his prime concerns, and it hadn't been a topic in his prayers. His mother's response was, "Well, you should, Son; it will be the most important decision you will ever make." He concluded, "As parents, we can teach our children to pray for things of eternal consequence—to pray for the strength to be morally clean in a very challenging world, to be obedient, and to have the courage to stand for the right."[27] Teens face tremendous pressures and can benefit from a parent's spiritual insights.

Helping Children Recognize Answers

Finally, parents should teach their children to pray to receive and then to follow divine guidance. As children grow older encourage them to pray for answers and trust what they receive.

I have a friend whose young daughter was struggling with a friendship that wasn't uplifting to her. My friend watched with concern before suggesting her daughter pray about this particular friendship. Through her prayers the daughter eventually recognized she needed to make some changes in the relationship so she could continue growing in healthy ways. Her life was blessed by a mother who encouraged her to pray over her personal concerns.

Another friend had a daughter who was at a crossroads in her education, and her parents encouraged her to pray for direction. When the daughter prayed she received an answer that was different from what she wanted, but she still had the strength to follow her impression. What an incredible opportunity to build spiritual stamina at a young age as she sought, received, and had the courage to follow revelation!

Elder Jeffrey R. Holland's son Matthew recalled a time when his father encouraged him to receive his own inspiration at the tender age of seven. Traveling down a series of dirt roads, close to dusk, father and son came to a

---

27 Tad R. Callister, "Parents: The Prime Gospel Teachers of Their Children," *Ensign*, Nov. 2014, 33.

fork in the road and didn't know which way to go. With daylight fading quickly it was imperative they make the right choice. Elder Holland, then a young father, turned to his son and suggested they pray. After the prayer he asked Matt what he thought, and Matt said he had received a distinct impression they should turn left. Elder Holland had received the same answer, so they turned left and drove for a few minutes before reaching a dead end. Quickly they turned around and sped back in the other direction. After a few minutes young Matt asked his dad why they had both received the answer to go left when it turned out to be a dead end. His dad responded, "The Lord has taught us an important lesson today. Because we were prompted to take the road to the left, we quickly discovered which one was the right one. When we turned around and got on the right road, I was able to travel along its many unfamiliar twists and turnoffs perfectly confident I was headed in the right direction.

"If we had started on the right road, we might have driven for 30 minutes or so, become uneasy with the unfamiliar surroundings, and been tempted to turn back. If we had done that, we would have discovered the dead-end so late that it would have been too dark to find our way back in totally unfamiliar territory." Elder Holland taught his son that sometimes the Lord will lead us in one direction as a means of getting us to the right end goal. Matthew Holland said, "I understood and have never forgotten the lesson my Heavenly Father and earthly father taught me that afternoon."[28] Life lessons about counseling with the Lord, listening for the Spirit, and receiving revelation were all learned because a father offered his son the opportunity to ask and listen for the Spirit.

What questions or concerns might you encourage your children to take to their Heavenly Father for answers? Parents who teach their children to ask for, expect, and follow revelation prepare them to receive their own testimonies and walk relying on their own light. This spiritual self-reliance is one of the greatest gifts we can give our children.

When threads of prayer are woven throughout the fabric of a family, faith, love, and unity are established. Parents set the tone by praying often, sincerely, and deeply. More threads are woven as parents make family prayer a "nonnegotiable priority"[29] and properly arm their children for the day. The fabric becomes strong as parents teach children to pray individually every morning and evening, exercise faith, and receive answers. Year after year your prayers can unify, bind your family together, and build eternal relationships.

---

28 Matthew Holland, "Wrong Roads and Revelation," *New Era*, July 2005, 27–28.
29 Richard G. Scott, "Make the Exercise of Faith Your First Priority," *Ensign*, Nov. 2014, 93.

Application

1. Work on the quality of your personal prayers. Do your prayers get the time and thought they need? Do you feel like you have communion with God?
2. Consider keeping a prayer journal. Jot down items you need to counsel with the Lord about as well as inspiration you receive.
3. Occasionally at dinner or other appropriate times share experiences when God answered your prayers.
4. How are your family prayers? Counsel as a family and discuss ways your family prayers could improve.
5. Occasionally inquire after your children's prayers. Do they pray regularly? Do they feel they receive answers?
6. Are there concerns you can pray with your children about so they can feel your love and support?
7. Consider keeping a family prayer list of people your family could regularly pray for.
8. Look for opportunities to encourage children to receive and follow personal revelation.

CHAPTER 4
Repentance

Joy is one of the inherent results of repentance. —Dale G. Renlund[1]

Do you remember holding your child as a newborn baby—tiny, precious, pure, and with that wonderful baby smell? When I held my oldest child those first few hours and days after his birth, I wanted to love, teach, encourage, and raise him to be a strong, courageous disciple of Christ. I certainly didn't want to make any mistakes. But, like most parents, I hadn't been home from the hospital for long when I realized parenting sometimes exacts more than I have to give and offers countless opportunities to repent, apologize, and keep trying.

When our fourth child was born, I posted a letter to her on my blog. It read in part:

> Sometimes I wonder what those wise blue eyes of yours see when they see me.
>
> Do you see straight through my soul? Do you see a mother who is painfully human and much more flawed than she likes? Sometimes I wonder if you do. It is a humbling assignment to give birth to yet another precious life. I wish so much that I could be a perfect mother. I wish I were perfectly patient, perfectly loving, and perfectly compassionate all the time. But I'm not. Do you see that when you look at me? Do you see someone who is just trying to cope through some moments?
>
> At other moments do you see someone who is completely in love with her children and with motherhood? I can't believe

---

1 Dale G. Renlund, "Repentance: A Joyful Choice," *Ensign*, Nov. 2016, 122.

how lucky I am to have four precious children. I am so grateful
we have each one of you and so grateful you have each other.
Families are forever—I am yours, you are mine, we are each
other's. What a gift!

Yes, children are gifts. Families are gifts. And some of the most important
gifts we as parents can give our families are the gifts of a pure heart, a contrite
spirit, and a family culture of apologizing and repenting. Oh, the opportunities
we have in our families to repent! When parents set the tone for this family
culture by apologizing when they mess up, they can keep their family united
with flames of love glowing brightly. Consider the power of this promise from
President Joseph F. Smith: "If you will keep your [children] close to your
heart, within the clasp of your arms; if you will make them to feel that you
love them . . . and keep them near to you, they will not go very far from you,
and they will not commit any very great sin. . . . If you wish your children to
be taught in the principles of the gospel, if you wish them to love the truth
and understand it, if you wish them to be obedient to and united with you,
love them! And prove to them that you do love them by your every word or
act to them."[2] Showing genuine love for our children is the best way to keep
them close to us, obedient, and faithful. Of course, we are all human. When
our efforts fall short of our goals, we must repent and apologize. Repenting
keeps hearts open and allows our children and families to feel safe, close, and
united with us.

Parental Repentance
It is hard to apologize, humbly admit fault, and repent, isn't it? Sometimes
as parents we don't do it enough. Maybe we don't want to admit to our family
members we were wrong. Maybe we don't feel like apologizing. Maybe we
worry about being seen as flawed because we admitted a fault. Maybe we
just get busy, move on, and forget other people might not be feeling loved
or whole because of our actions. As much as possible it's best to apologize
immediately, before too much damage has accrued. Other times the Spirit
might prompt you during an evening prayer about an incident that needs an
apology. Apologize quickly. You will notice you will feel better and so will your
children. Parental apologies teach children they are loved and their parents are
trustworthy.

---

2 *Teachings of Presidents of the Church: Joseph F. Smith* (1998), 253–54.

Repentance Keeps the Spirit

In addition to keeping family harmony and trust intact, apologizing to our family members when needed keeps us in tune with the Spirit. Having the Spirit is essential to good parenting. The Spirit can prompt us to know how to protect, guide, love, and encourage our children.

Once when President Harold B. Lee was young, a mighty thunderstorm was raging near his family's home. Harold, his mother, his grandmother, and a few siblings sat clustered in the doorway watching nature's powerful display. Suddenly Harold's mother pushed him hard and sent him reeling out the doorway. Immediately afterward a bolt of lightning came down the chimney, shot out the doorway where Harold had been sitting, and split a huge gash in the tree in front of their home. Later in his adulthood Harold saw the tree, which still bore the scar from that night, and felt tremendous gratitude for a mother who was in tune with the Spirit and was prepared to protect him from danger.[3]

As parents we may or may not be privy to the details of how we have protected our children. Often the dangers surrounding us will not be as physically obvious or ever-present as a scarred tree in our front yard. But we know living our lives in tune with the Spirit of the Lord is critical if we are to protect our families and live clean lives in a world of moral danger.

The Prophet Joseph Smith had an experience that taught him about the connection between repentance and keeping the Spirit. When Joseph was translating the Book of Mormon, he got upset with Emma one morning over something that had happened at home. Shortly afterward Joseph went upstairs to begin working on the translation and found he couldn't. As long as he was harboring feelings of anger or frustration the Spirit couldn't guide him in the translation process. He went outside and prayed for about an hour, came back to ask Emma's forgiveness, and then was able to resume the translation.[4]

How might the same principle apply in parenting? If we yell or are harsh with our children, the Spirit is grieved. The more quickly we apologize for our actions and show our love for our children, the more quickly we can have the Spirit with us.

Leading by Example

Apologizing requires us to swallow our pride and admit our fault, and that is hard to do. Sometimes we might fool ourselves into thinking our family

---

3 Blaine M. Yorgason, *Humble Servant, Spiritual Giant: The Story of Harold B. Lee* (2001), 29–31.

4 *Teachings of Presidents of the Church: Joseph Smith* (2007), 116.

members didn't notice our fault. Sometimes we may feel tempted to justify our actions. Of course, as we gain experience as parents—and perhaps as we recall our own experiences growing up—we realize family members notice and will often forgive without being asked. But openly repenting demonstrates that we hold ourselves to the same standard we exact of our children. Parental repentance can foster trust and deepen love.

President Heber J. Grant's daughter Frances shared an example of this principle. When she was a child, she had used some inappropriate language. Her father washed her mouth out with soap, said that her mouth was clean, and admonished her not to make it dirty again with bad language.

A few days later Frances heard her father tell a story and quote the profane language the person in the story had used. Immediately she pointed out the discrepancy—if she wasn't allowed to use such language, he shouldn't either.

Many parents in this scenario might feel tempted to hedge or rationalize their behavior. But if we are to demonstrate pure hearts and intentions for our children, we must hold ourselves to the same standard we use for them.

In this instance President Grant was humble enough to recognize his error. He agreed with Frances and asked if she would like to wash his mouth out. She did. And she noticed that after that he never quoted others' colorful language again. She said, "From that moment I knew that my father would be absolutely fair in all his dealings with me, and I never found him otherwise."[5]

Do you apologize quickly and frequently enough to show your children you are trustworthy?

Repentance Teaches Children Their Worth

Frances's experience hints at another important aspect of parental apologies. When parents apologize to their children, they teach children their worth. Children are not objects for parents to occasionally stomp on or disregard. Adults sometimes request apologies of others. Children are young and are learning how to process their feelings, and they often don't know to ask for an apology when they are hurt. When young children are apologized to, they learn that their needs and feelings matter. They learn that even adults make mistakes and when they do they apologize. Sometimes parents can get overwhelmed with all the needs that press on them. It is easy for parents to rationalize their behavior and convince themselves that their actions are okay. Taking a step back from a situation to own personal responsibility and talk openly to your child requires humility. But humility teaches a child that a parent can be trusted.

5 *Teachings of Presidents of the Church: Heber J. Grant* (2002), xvi–xviii.

Elder Jeffrey R. Holland's wife, Pat, shared an experience with repentance she had with her daughter, Mary. Mary had demonstrated musical talent in her youth, and Pat worried about helping her magnify that talent. Over time a pattern of Pat closely supervising Mary's piano practice developed, and their relationship began to suffer. Wrestling with fears that Mary's talent might go undeveloped or that her relationship with Mary might continue to deteriorate, Pat prayed for guidance. Finally, three days before Christmas, she presented Mary with an early present—an apron with the strings cut off. Tucked in a pocket of the apron was a note apologizing for any problems she may have caused and expressing her concern, confidence, and love. Years later Mary told Pat that her apology had filled her with a great sense of worth, showing her that sometimes children can be right and adults can be wrong, and demonstrating that she was worthy of her parent's apology.[6]

Choosing Love over Fear

The Hollands' experience is an appropriate example of something that typically happens in parenting. Often our greatest hopes and our deepest fears center in our families. If a child's behavior is concerning, the parents' first instincts are often to crack down, lecture, inform, and spew out threats or consequences. It is instructive to note that our Heavenly Father chooses to motivate with love. When we feel the Spirit, we feel love, peace, joy, and hope. If we choose to question or doubt, fear can overwhelm us. Fear is a prime tool of the adversary.

How do we parent out of love instead of fear? Take a step back and consider what your specific concerns are. Pray about them. Go to the temple. Ask the Lord to help you see your child through His eyes, with divine talents and potential. Soak in the feelings of hope, peace, and love the Spirit can bring. Then share your heart with your child. Instead of poisoning relationships with threats, it is better to express love and confidence. Express your concerns, share your hopes and dreams, and bring your child into the warmth of your love. Sharing your innermost feelings and apologizing for previous tactics that might not have been the best makes it easier for children to feel safe and close to parents.

Are there aspects of your parenting in which fear grabs hold of your heart? Could repenting, apologizing, and expressing love and confidence help heal your relationships with your children? Love and faith conquer fear. Express love. Demonstrate love. Pray for love. When you are filled with the love of

---

6 Patricia T. Holland, "Parenting: Everything to Do with the Heart," *Ensign*, June 1985, 14.

our Heavenly Father and Savior, you will feel hope, confidence, and faith. The closer you draw to the Lord, the further fear will dissipate and you will be able to share His love with your family.

As you strive to follow the Savior in your parenting you will recognize the value of meekness. Our children and families are not our possessions—they are a priceless stewardship. Openly apologizing when we need to shows our children our pure determination to follow Christ and helps them feel safe and secure in our love.

Encouraging Children to Repent
Starting Young or Starting Now

It is important for parents to set the example by apologizing to their children when necessary—but every parent knows that's only part of the battle. It is equally essential for parents to teach their children to repent and apologize to each other. It's best to start these habits when children are young. If your children are older and you haven't established a family culture of repentance and forgiveness—or if you feel your family's repentance habits could use a little tune-up—gather your family for a family council. Explain your concerns and your goals: families are eternal, and you want your family to love each other and be friends now and in the eternities. Part of reaching that goal involves frequently repenting and forgiving each other. Tell your children you will be working to apologize when necessary yourself. Ask for their cooperation to do the same. You might even role play what a good apology looks and sounds like. Explain that they might need to ask you to repent, and you might need to ask them to repent as you all establish new habits. But express confidence that you can all accomplish it together and be a stronger, more united family. When goals are shared in a spirit of love, it will be easier to get your family on board and make meaningful changes. Follow up as appropriate until good habits are more firmly entrenched.

Teach your children to apologize to each other. In our home, when our children quarrel, we have them sit down together to apologize and tell each other what they should have done differently. We try not to focus on finding fault or casting blame. Everyone is human and imperfect, and no one feels good having their flaws magnified. By citing what they should have done instead, we hope to teach our children to look forward and realize what they could do in the same situation in the future. Then we ask them to hug each other and express love. If hurt feelings or pouting persist after this, it sometimes helps to take a child aside with a hug and a brief chat about the value of forgiveness.

If one or more children have done something unusually hurtful or wrong, we might encourage them to make restitution to the sibling who was wronged. Allowing children to choose what they will do to make restitution teaches them about love, sorrow, and repentance. Left to choose, our children have come up with simple solutions, such as sharing a toy, writing a loving note, or doing a chore, that are satisfactory to both parties.

Praying with Them

It is worth noting that not all incidents prompting repentance can be handled quickly or smoothly. Sometimes children aren't penitent and don't want to discuss the issue or repent. If your child is not ready to plop right down and discuss the problem, consider what you might do to show more love and help soften her heart.

At one point during the Prophet Joseph Smith's life, his younger brother William became upset over one of Joseph's decisions. William was openly antagonistic toward the Prophet Joseph, and he was encouraging others to follow suit. One day William, Joseph Smith Sr., and a few others went to Joseph's house. In the presence of those gathered, Father Smith opened with a prayer and then expressed to his sons his concern over their current difficulties. Joseph recorded, "the Spirit of God rested down upon us in mighty power, and our hearts were melted." William confessed his fault and asked forgiveness, and Joseph did the same.[7]

What power prayer can have to purify hearts and bring change in families and relationships! On occasion, when there are squabbles in our home, I like to take the antagonists aside. Sometimes this means all of my children need to be involved, and sometimes I will choose just one child whose attitude is particularly suffering. I will pray and express my love for each child and my desires for harmony and an eternal family unit. After that I invite my children to pray as well. Sometimes they still don't want to, and I don't force the issue. I then like to express love and confidence. I might tell them how glad we are that they are in our family, that I know the Lord can help them be kind to each other, and that I am glad they will always have each other as siblings and friends.

Praying with children who need to repent is a poignant way of sharing your heart and innermost desires with them. When children feel your love and the Spirit of the Lord, they are more likely to want to repent and have the Holy Ghost in their lives too.

---

7 *Teachings of Presidents of the Church: Joseph Smith* (2007), 395–96.

Teaching Doctrine

In addition to praying with children and helping them repent, it is helpful to consider what doctrines or values you might help them internalize to improve their actions in the future. Would a family home evening lesson on love or thoughtfulness help? Could you recognize and encourage positive actions of selflessness to help family harmony improve? Does your child understand the importance of integrity or courage in standing up for what's right? When taught through the Spirit, doctrine can change our children's hearts and natures. Family units provide critical opportunities to teach and discuss these doctrines. Plan an appropriate family night, discuss a story with an applicable value over dinner, and start giving the doctrine a bit more air time around your home.

It is also important to weigh the gravity of your child's actions. President Dallin H. Oaks has taught, "Both sins and mistakes can hurt us and both require attention, but the scriptures direct a different treatment. . . . Violations of the commandments of God are sins that require chastening and repentance."[8] Sometimes a problem can be fixed with an apology. Sometimes restitution is needed. Occasionally more prolonged repentance is in order.

When a child's errors are deep sins, it is easy for parents to feel a range of emotions such as fear, anger, and betrayal. It is especially important at these times to correct and teach with love so the Spirit can soften your child's heart while you discuss doctrine. It is also important to consider whether you have adequately taught your children. Do they understand the why of the doctrine? The more we can help children feel the Savior's love and understand the beauty of His teachings, the more success we are likely to have. When doctrine is understood, it can change your child's heart.

Alma's words to his son Corianton in Alma 39 through 42 are a perfect example of this principle of effective teaching. Corianton had failed to focus on his mission to the Zoramites and had been distracted by the harlot Isabel. Alma responded by first explaining the gravity of Corianton's sin before clearing up some of Corianton's doctrinal misconceptions regarding the Fall, Atonement, and Resurrection. It is significant to note that while teaching Corianton, Alma shared his own testimony and taught things he personally had learned through spiritual inquiry (see Alma 3, 11). How often do we sincerely teach and bear testimony to our children? Do our children know of the spiritual experiences we have had, the questions we have asked, and the answers we have received? Lovingly bearing testimony to a struggling child may help the child feel love

---

8 Dallin H. Oaks, "Sins and Mistakes," *Ensign*, Oct. 1996, 62.

and hope. Alma's efforts to teach and clarify the doctrine for Corianton were successful; a few chapters later we read about Corianton diligently teaching the gospel among the Nephites (see Alma 49:30).

How might lovingly teaching doctrine and bearing testimony help a child who is struggling with sin or error?

President Joseph Fielding Smith's son Reynolds recalled an instance when his father caught him in sin and corrected with love and true doctrine. When Reynolds was in junior high, he had a friend who smoked and often encouraged him to try it. One day as Reynolds and his friend were leaving school, Reynolds finally caved to his friend's pressure—he took a cigarette, lit it, and took a couple of puffs. Just then his father pulled up to the curb. Rolling down his window, Joseph Fielding Smith told his astonished son he wanted to talk to him that night after dinner.

After dinner, Reynolds and his father retired to his father's study. Joseph Fielding Smith lovingly reminded him about the dangers of cigarettes and elicited a promise that Reynolds would never smoke again. Reynolds never did.[9]

In our home we have worked to apply principles of love and repentance with our children. At one point one of our daughters was having some honesty issues. After the first episode I sat down with her to talk about what had happened and what should have been different. We read and discussed some scriptures, and I expressed my love and confidence in her. I felt really good about the encounter. Two days later when I caught her lying again, I felt betrayed and wondered how our previous discussion hadn't had any lasting effect. I waited a few hours to calm down, talk to Cameron, and feel ready to talk to our daughter again. It is easy at times like this to think of harsh penalties, but integrity is an important issue. We wanted to help our daughter truly desire to change rather than to simply provide external consequences to produce a short-term episode of repentance. That evening I asked what she thought would help her do better. She suggested she could pray every morning for help to be honest. She made a sign to post by her bed as a reminder. In the coming weeks I occasionally would ask if she was remembering to pray about honesty. I continued to express confidence and encouragement and was pleased to see her becoming much more honest and trustworthy. Months later, when those lying episodes were long in the past, I noticed her flowered honesty sign still hanging above her bed. I was pleased that she instinctively understood she needed to turn to the Lord for the strength and help she needed.

---

9 *Teachings of the Presidents of the Church: Joseph Fielding Smith* (2013), 181–83.

Loving and Encouraging

Inherent throughout the process of praying with our children and teaching them doctrine is the need for love and encouragement. If your child has erred, he needs to feel your love and know there is hope for his repentance. Children need to know you still love them and trust them to do better. Parents can do much to provide a safe environment for their children's repentance. If children know they will be loved and encouraged rather than condemned and criticized, it will be easier for them to apologize and make amends and feel good about what they have learned.

President Joseph F. Smith's son Willard was once bullied by another boy. Willard responded by making the bully a "valentine" full of every harsh, vituperative word he could conceive. He accidentally put the bully's valentine in the wrong envelope, the one he'd addressed for his uncle's valentine. The valentine intended for the bully went to Willard's uncle and eventually ended up on his father's desk. The next morning at family prayer Joseph told Willard to come to his office, opened a large Bible, turned to a few verses about forgiving and not swearing, and let Willard read them. Finally he hugged and kissed him, and that was the end of the discussion. Willard never used another bad word.[10]

Sometimes parents need to correct their children and share doctrinal reminders. Couching these experiences with affection and encouragement makes it easier for children to bounce back and return to good habits. The scriptures urge us to "[show] forth afterwards an increase of love" (D&C 121:43) when we correct someone. When children can make mistakes, learn, and still feel confident in your love and their worth, they can feel freer to grow and progress in the way our Father in Heaven has designed.

Teaching doctrine to our children enough to let it truly soak into their hearts and souls is the process of a lifetime. We might notice an issue, prepare a wonderful family home evening lesson, and still keep experiencing the same problem. Take heart and keep loving, working, and encouraging. Changing to become more like Christ takes time and effort. At times we may feel like throwing our hands in the air and walking away. It is helpful to remember that no matter how many times we fall, our Father in Heaven, our Savior, and the Holy Ghost are willing to keep striving with us. We must offer the same grace to others.

Worldly parenting books are full of quick fixes, promising easy solutions for everything from getting babies to sleep to teaching older kids to be obedient

---

10 Truman G. Madsen, *The Presidents of the Church: Insights into Their Lives and Teachings* (2004), 159–60.

and hardworking. These options sound good and attract attention. But the gospel is not a quick fix, and neither is teaching our children. We can throw consequences at a problem, but what we really need is to teach, train, and apply gospel principles. Love, service, courage, integrity, patience, gratitude, faith, and selflessness aren't quick fixes either. However, they are the answers to a lot of glitches in family harmony. Have faith in your children. Keep trying, keep repenting, and let them keep trying too.

Application

1. Take each of your children aside individually. Ask if you apologize to them enough. Set a goal to genuinely apologize as often as needed. Make it a consistent item in your daily prayers.

2. Call a family council and discuss goals to have a better family culture of repenting and forgiving. Occasionally role play what a good apology looks and sounds like.

3. When there is a problem to be addressed, take the child aside for a moment of prayer and loving encouragement.

4. Make a list of doctrines that might merit a family home evening lesson to improve behaviors in the family.

5. Start gathering a file of stories that illustrate specific doctrines or values you want to share with your family. Occasionally share and discuss a story during family dinner.

6. If you are worried about a particular child's behavior, share your heart with your child. Express your love, concerns, and confidence.

7. Set a goal to always show an increase of love after correcting a child. Pray about it and discuss with the Lord individual incidences to find ways to improve.

8. Bear your testimony of specific doctrines that need a bit more focus. Share things you have learned through your own experiences.

CHAPTER 5
Forgiveness

If, when we have difficulties one with another, we would be kind and affable to each other, we would save ourselves a great deal of trouble.
—Wilford Woodruff[1]

ALL FAMILIES HAVE CHALLENGES AND flaws. God sent us to families so we could learn about the Christlike attributes of love and sacrifice but also so we could practice Christlike virtues of forgiveness and repentance. We love our family members more deeply than we love most other people, and that love opens us up to deeper levels of hurt, disappointment, and betrayal when our loved ones make choices we don't like. How we choose to respond to the daily small—and occasionally large—grievances will determine much of the love, joy, and happiness our families enjoy.

As with other aspects of family life, forgiveness in our families paints the landscape for our posterity in generations to come. President Gordon B. Hinckley explained, "As children grow through the years, their lives, in large measure, become an extension and a reflection of family teaching. . . . As mercy is given and taught by parents, it will be repeated in the lives and actions of the next generation."[2] How we love and forgive in our marriages and parenting teaches our children how to love and forgive each other through the inevitable sibling squabbles that occur. How quickly we overlook and move beyond the mistakes our children make teaches them about love, mercy, and forgiveness.

Sometimes we might look at other families at church or on social media and assume we are alone in our constant need to forgive each other. It's helpful to remember that we might not know the full story behind other people's lives. Everyone makes mistakes, and everyone requires forgiveness, whether or not

1 *Teachings of Presidents of the Church: Wilford Woodruff* (2004), 168.
2 *Teachings of Presidents of the Church: Gordon B. Hinckley* (2016), 174.

we are privy to the details in other families' situations. President Gordon B. Hinckley's children recalled a scenario that happens in many families. When their family would drive out of town for family vacation, car piled high with family members and all their gear, they couldn't reach the city limits before typical sibling bickering ensued. At this point President Hinckley, then a young father, would pull the car over to the side of the road and proclaim, "We are going home *right now* if you can't get along with each other."[3] It's not a scenario most mention in their Christmas cards, but it's typical of many families. Even the Prophet Joseph Smith, with his tremendous calling and spiritual abilities, wasn't impervious to occasional human folly. At one point the Prophet Joseph turned to his secretary Howard Coray and playfully challenged him to a little wrestling match. Unfortunately, somehow in the tussle, the prophet broke Brother Coray's leg. Full of remorse Joseph carried him home and carefully ministered to him.[4]

All of us, parents and children, are subject to occasional human mistakes and lacking judgment. All of us need to forgive and be forgiven. How do we respond when the going gets tough with our children? If I were to compile a cursory list of my children's typical grievances that require forgiveness, it would become immediately clear that in each instance, responding with love, mercy, and forgiveness would yield a better long-term relationship. I can choose to proclaim in exasperation, "How many times have I told you?" and create a rift between me and my children—and teach them bad habits to imitate in the future—or I can exercise patience as I work through my frustration. As the Prophet Joseph Smith taught, "Nothing is so much calculated to lead people to forsake sin as to take them by the hand, and watch over them with tenderness. When persons manifest the least kindness and love to me, O what power it has over my mind, while the opposite course has a tendency to harrow up all the harsh feelings and depress the human mind. . . . There should be no license for sin, but mercy should go hand in hand with reproof."[5]

Extending mercy to our children, spouse, and others can mean swallowing harsh responses, praying for a spirit of love, and reaching out with tenderness to correct and teach. It can also mean choosing to let some offenses go, using discretion, and maintaining a sense of humor. Above all, it should include daily personal strivings to diligently study and emulate the life of our Savior Jesus Christ. The more we become like Him, the more natural it will be to

---

3 Sheri L. Dew, *Go Forward with Faith: The Biography of Gordon B. Hinckley* (1996), 167.

4 Truman G. Madsen, *Joseph Smith the Prophet* (1989), 31.

5 Joseph Smith, *History of the Church, Volume 5* (Salt Lake City: Deseret Book, 1980), 23–24.

respond in love when we are disappointed in others. As the Prophet Joseph Smith taught, "The nearer we get to our heavenly Father, the more we are disposed to look with compassion on perishing souls; we feel that we want to take them upon our shoulders, and cast their sins behind our backs."[6] Working to develop Christlike attributes will pave the way for us to forgive more quickly and respond more lovingly.

Forgiving Quickly

Family life runs more smoothly when everyone works to forgive quickly. Helping children learn to forgive each other promptly can take consistent effort, and the example of a parent can make a big difference. President Joseph F. Smith's daughter Edith Eleanor was impressed by her father's example in this regard. Joseph F. Smith was heavily persecuted by the media, and once when Edith Eleanor went to school, she found people there with "false reports and lies" about her father. Feeling understandably upset as she saw the father she loved being misrepresented, she confronted him about it and asked why he didn't do something. "You're not doing one thing, and these mean men are taking advantage of you, printing all these lies, and you don't do one thing about it!" Joseph F. Smith gently smiled and explained that the people who spread lies only hurt themselves.[7]

How do your children see you respond when offense is given? How quickly do you forgive those around you, particularly your family members? Elder Dieter F. Uchtdorf of the Quorum of the Twelve Apostles said, "I have discovered one thing that most [happy families] have in common: they have a way of forgiving and forgetting the imperfections of others and looking for the good."[8] Setting a tone of lighthearted forgiveness creates a happier home.

Anger Is a Choice

How can we establish a habit of forgiving quickly? It might be worth taking a quick personal analysis to consider the example that is set in your home. When your children misbehave, how do you respond? How often do you choose anger? How long do you allow such feelings to linger? Elder Lynn G. Robbins of the Seventy has taught, "No one makes us mad. Others don't make us angry. There is no force involved. Becoming angry is a conscious choice, a decision; therefore, we can make the choice not to become angry. *We* choose!"[9]

---

6 *Teachings of Presidents of the Church: Joseph Smith* (2007), 428–29.
7 *Teachings of Presidents of the Church: Joseph F. Smith* (2013), 257.
8 Dieter F. Uchtdorf, "One Key to a Happy Family," *Ensign*, Oct. 2012, 5.
9 Lynn G. Robbins, "Agency and Anger," *Ensign*, May 1998, 80, emphasis in original.

If you frequently feel angry with your children, please do not throw this book down and declare yourself a lost cause. Part of parenthood is facing nearly insurmountable odds—difficult temperaments, taxing behavior problems, challenging circumstances—and learning how to respond. If you feel angry, you are not alone. And there is hope. Remember the counsel from Ether 12:27, where the Lord tells us, "If men come unto me I will show unto them their weakness. I give unto men weakness that they may be humble; and my grace is sufficient for all men that humble themselves before me; for if they humble themselves before me, and have faith in me, then will I make weak things become strong unto them." Parenthood has a stunning way of helping us see our weaknesses, doesn't it? But there is hope and help for each of us—anger, weaknesses, and all—because of the grace of Jesus Christ.

Learning to choose a response other than anger takes time, diligent effort, and reliance on the Savior. Consistently praying for strength and planning how you will respond in different situations is a first step. When you blow it, apologize quickly. Pray about what happened, and ask the Lord to inspire you with what you should have done and can do differently in the future. Ask for the strength to respond with greater forgiveness. Talk through possible scenarios with a spouse or close friend. Above all, don't give up because of a bad day or a bad series of days! Everyone has them. We achieve success only as we keep trying to improve.

Eventually it becomes clear that anger only impedes progress. Anger is a secondary emotion. Often the first emotion you feel is hurt, sadness, or disappointment. Conveying these first emotions to family members—along with deep love—can help you forgive more quickly. Additionally, sharing sadness and love, rather than anger, with family members makes it easier for the other person to quickly repent and change.

President Thomas S. Monson recalled observing his father's choice of calm over anger in a humorous incident. One day young Tommy and a friend set out on a little neighborhood mission to gather stray dogs. Once they had captured the dogs they decided the best place to keep them would be in Tommy's coal shed. When Tommy's father got home from work he went out to the shed to fill the coal bucket. As the door swung open he was greeted by six hostage dogs who were eager to be free. President Monson recalled, "Dad flushed a little bit, and then he calmed down and quietly told me, 'Tommy, coal sheds are for coal. Other people's dogs rightfully belong to them.'"[10]

I love the way President Monson's father chose to stay calm. I think it is particularly instructive that he corrected his son quietly. When a parent feels

---

10 Heidi S. Swinton, *To the Rescue: The Biography of Thomas S. Monson* (2010), 35.

like yelling but chooses to whisper or use a quiet voice instead, the parent maintains personal control and the child's respect for the parent can grow. I have found that whispering or lowering my voice at critical moments is perhaps even more effective than using a louder voice to get my child's attention. A lowered voice signals to children that the topic is important and they should listen. Yelling demonstrates a lack of respect and teaches children to tune out. As President Gordon B. Hinckley taught, "We seldom get into trouble when we speak softly."[11]

Maintaining Perspective

We can replace the choice to become angry with other conscious choices. When our children's choices disappoint us, sometimes it is helpful to consider the situation through the child's eyes. Before drawing our own conclusions, we can assume good. Pause long enough to ask yourself if there is a possibility for a child's behavior other than defiance, irresponsibility, or malevolence. Refusing to jump to negative conclusions can keep the bridge of communication open.

Elder Jeffrey R. Holland's son Matthew shared a story from his childhood, when his mother was able to maintain perspective and forgive quickly and sincerely. Matthew was running outside to play, and his mother emphasized the fact that he should not come back in with muddy feet because she was washing and waxing the floor. He recalled playing outside for probably an hour or so before running happily back inside with very muddy feet. Halfway across the gleaming clean floor, when he realized his transgression, he quickly darted for the bedroom, burst into tears, and buried his face in his pillow.

What would you do at this point? Loudly complain as you reclean the floor? Reprimand your child? Or take a deep breath and remember that little boys' memories don't hold details about clean floors for very long?

Matthew heard the door open and glanced over to see his mother. "Mom, you don't love me!" he cried out. She quickly responded, "I *do* love you, and I'll do anything to prove it!" She then picked up his muddy feet and kissed them. He recalls, "Needless to say, that experience taught me a great deal about the meaning of repentance and forgiveness."[12]

I love this example of quick forgiveness and this mother's ability to keep life in perspective. Children are more important than clean floors, and they need to know and feel that.

Along with considering incidents through the eyes of your children (with their current capacities), it helps to look at the big picture. Sometimes children

---

11 *Teachings of Presidents of the Church: Gordon B. Hinckley* (2016), 174.
12 Matthew Holland, "Muddy Feet and White Shirts," *Ensign*, May 1983, 38–39.

bring home bigger disasters than muddy feet. Keeping your cool in these times, showing love, and forgiving quickly keeps doors of communication open. Kids make mistakes. Parents make mistakes. Say a prayer in the moment, and try to remember we all learn and grow and sometimes the process is awkward and messy. Forgiving each other quickly allows others to stumble, recover, and keep progressing.

Cooling Down

While heralding the virtue of forgiving quickly, it is worth gently confessing the fact that sometimes forgiving quickly is hard. At times it's best to take a step back and calm down before instructing or interacting with our children. When President Gordon B. Hinckley was a young father and one of his children's actions was particularly irksome, he went outside to prune the trees until he felt calmer.[13] (I love that mental image. It seems like the perfect cool-down activity.) If you need time to calm down, choose something constructive to help you feel better. Hopping online to pass time until you feel better can be mind- and soul-numbing. Praying, calling your spouse or a close friend, listening to inspiring music, writing down feelings in a notebook to help you sort through things, or reading something uplifting can help you feel better more quickly and productively.

Consider what you are feeling and why. Underneath an initial angry impulse are deeper feelings such as hurt, fear, betrayal of trust, or disappointment at unmet expectations. What are you really feeling deep down inside? How can you address this concern and resolve the issue with your child?

When you take a few minutes to step back and prayerfully consider an aggravating situation, you can retain the respect of your children and the harmony in your home. President Joseph F. Smith stated, "The man that will be angry at his boy, and try to correct him while he is in anger, is in the greatest fault. . . . You can only correct your children by love, in kindness, by love unfeigned, by persuasion, and reason."[14] Another time he taught, "For your own sake, for the love that should exist between you and your [children] . . . when you speak or talk to them, do it not in anger, do it not harshly, in a condemning spirit. Speak to them kindly. . . . Soften their hearts; get them to feel tenderly toward you."[15] Sometimes taking a few quiet moments enables us to think more clearly and respond to our children more lovingly. Cooling

13 Sheri L. Dew, *Go Forward with Faith: The Biography of Gordon B. Hinckley* (1996), 170.
14 *Teachings of Presidents of the Church: Joseph F. Smith* (1998), 254.
15 *Teachings of the Presidents of the Church: Joseph F. Smith*, 254.

down also allows us to keep the Spirit with us and prevents us from damaging our relationships.

Taking Time to Teach

While you are taking a few moments to feel calm, another important matter to consider is your children's viewpoints. Do they understand why what they did was wrong? Is there a clarification of a doctrine or principle that might help them steer their course in another direction? For instance, if there is too much quarreling between siblings, a family home evening lesson or family dinner discussions about selflessness might help. Parents must constantly teach and model gospel principles they want their children to absorb.

Choose to love your child and ask open-ended questions to help you gain insights into their level of understanding. Sometimes children might not have a stunning answer for such questions. Pray for discernment. It helps to remember experiences from your own childhood, when you appreciated mercy and forgiveness. The world can be a big, uncertain place, especially for children and youth. We are all still learning, and we need to grant our children room to learn and grow. They can do this better if we forgive quickly.

Working to instill doctrines and values into the hearts of our children requires good examples and seemingly endless repetition from parents. I like the example of President Gordon B. Hinckley's father in this regard. Rather than lecturing his children, he liked to repeat favorite sayings that conveyed his expectations. Some of his were, "Be somebody. Stand up for something," and "Try to live up to the high-water mark of your possibilities."[16] When former Relief Society general president Louise Yates Robison was raising her children, she often repeated a few favorite maxims, such as, "Live above petty things; don't descend to their level," and "Welcome the task that takes you beyond yourself."[17] When Mary Ellen Smoot was growing up, her mother told her, "Whatever you do, do with your might, jobs done by halves are never done right."[18] Bonnie Parkin regularly heard her mother say, "Do what is right, let the consequences follow."[19] When I was growing up, my dad often quoted his grandmother with two of her favorite sayings: "If you can't say something nice, don't say anything at all," and "You catch more flies with honey than

16 Sheri L. Dew, *Go Forward with Faith: The Biography of Gordon B. Hinckley* (1996), 36.

17 Jane Peterson and LaRene Gaunt, *Faith, Hope, and Charity: Inspiration from the Lives of General Relief Society Presidents* (2008), 132.

18 Peterson and Gaunt, *Faith, Hope, and Charity*, 247.

19 Peterson and Gaunt, *Faith, Hope, and Charity,* 271.

you do with vinegar." Now I often repeat these sayings for my own children. Brief snippets of truth can convey values and expectations without the damage incurred by a lecture.

When Silence Is Golden

While considering what we might help our children understand, it is also helpful to consider the gravity of their actions. If their choices are sinful, parents should lovingly teach and help them work toward repentance. If their actions are irritating or inconsiderate, consider how to help them steer a better course. Loving correction may be first in order, administered in a spirit of patience and understanding. Extending mercy and understanding rather than criticism and condemnation while teaching your children will keep hearts and ears open. Perhaps in some situations nothing needs to be said for children to make their own conclusions about how to choose better. Children's mistakes can be frustrating at times and can require more patience than parents might feel capable of extending. As parents we often make mistakes and can only hope our children will offer us forgiveness and mercy as they reflect on our efforts. We all require each other's patience as we sometimes glide and other times blunder through life. Our children's love for us will increase as we extend patience, grace, and mercy to their learning curves.

Our Father in Heaven designed our mortal experience with a Savior so we could learn from our mistakes without being condemned by them.[20] Through the Atonement we can repent and keep trying and stumbling and learning to "prize the good" (Moses 6:55), and eventually we will become more like our Savior. We must extend the same opportunity of learning to our children.

President David O. McKay shared with his secretary Clare how learning to keep his cool when he was frustrated with others had happened over the course of a lifetime. Clare noticed she had never heard President McKay say anything unkind, even when the environment was potentially tense or offensive. She finally asked him why, and he explained, "I learned many years ago, when I felt a surge of anger or retort coming over me, to put my tongue way back in my mouth and clamp my teeth down on it, and not to say an unkind and hurtful thing. Every time that I did that, I found that it was easier the next time to control my feelings."[21] After this disclosure, whenever Clare noticed President McKay putting his tongue back in his mouth, she would smile and realize the pressures he must have felt as the prophet and president of the Church. The

---

20 Bruce C. Hafen, "The Atonement: All for All," *Ensign*, May 2004, 97.
21 Mary Jane Woodger, *David O. McKay: Beloved Prophet* (2004), 184.

same might be true of parents. Parents operate under incredible daily stresses. Careers, children's needs, financial struggles, Church service, and myriad other factors can sometimes make life seem nearly unbearable. President McKay's method would be helpful for just about any parent.

Another instance from the life of President David O. McKay illustrates a similar principle. When one of his sons was a teenager, face cards were somewhat of a taboo item, and the McKay family didn't own any. The McKays' son wanted to test his independence, so he bought some face cards and kept them in his room. When David O. McKay came in to look for something in his son's room, he found the cards and inquired who their owner was. The son confessed. David O. McKay simply looked at his son, put the cards back in the drawer, and walked out of the room. Another word was never said about it, but the son's conscience must have been pricked, because the cards disappeared soon after.[22]

Children who have been properly taught know what is expected of them. Perhaps little or nothing needs to be said for a child to recognize an error and correct it on her own. Sometimes a parent can enable quicker repentance by not making a big deal and by letting their children draw wisdom from their own mistakes.

President Harold B. Lee recalled a time when his father showed patience and mercy with his mistakes. Their family's pigs had been destroying the garden and causing havoc, and Harold's father sent him two miles into town to get a tool to help them ring the pigs' noses. Once he returned with the tool, father and son went to work to get all the pigs gathered in the pen. In the process, young Harold was playing with the tool, pushed down too hard, and broke it. His father simply looked at him, smiled, and said, "Well, son, I guess we won't ring the pigs today." President Lee went on to explain, "How I loved that father, that he didn't scold me for an innocent little mistake that could have made a breach between us."[23] President Lee's father was wise enough to know his son recognized his mistake and felt foolish. Keeping calm and not heaping correction allowed young Harold to maintain his dignity and his love for his father.

Sometimes children don't need us to point out their errors. Offering love and understanding and being content to let children learn their own lessons without our editorials may be the most gracious response.

---

22 Mary Jane Woodger, *David O. McKay: Beloved Prophet* (2004), 98–99.
23 *Teachings of Presidents of the Church: Harold B. Lee* (2000), 132–33.

Loving Unconditionally

At every step throughout the process of family altercations, and especially after correcting our children, it is critical that we "[show] forth afterwards an increase of love" (D&C 121:43). The concept of forgiving and loving is taught beautifully throughout the three parables the Savior shared in Luke 15. In the first parable one of the shepherd's one hundred sheep wanders off, perhaps in the innocent, unaware way sheep tend to do. The shepherd seeks out the sheep, rejoices when it is found, carries it home, and calls on his friends and neighbors to rejoice with him (see Luke 15:3–7). Our Father in Heaven is merciful when we stray, seeks after us, and will carry us home and rejoice that we are with Him. We should likewise reach out to our children with love and forgiveness.

In the next parable a woman loses one of her ten pieces of silver. She searches "diligently" until she finds it, just as our Father in Heaven works diligently to seek after His children who are lost (Luke 15:8). The Savior concludes this parable by saying, "Likewise, I say unto you, there is joy in the presence of the angels of God over one sinner that repenteth" (Luke 15:10). What a beautiful illustration of the love our Father has for us! When one of His children repents, He rejoices and so do those who are with Him. Our heavenly home is clearly a place of love where people work, encourage, and rejoice in the smallest successes of others. We can follow this heavenly pattern by forgiving, holding our tongues when we are disappointed, and encouraging family members in their best efforts.

The final parable of Luke 15 is the parable of the prodigal son. In this instance we see someone who willingly sins in ways that would have been deeply hurtful to his parents, including demanding his inheritance money while his father was still alive, leaving home, and spending his inheritance on "riotous living" (Luke 15:13). But when the son finally desires a change, he knows he is safe to go home. He knows his father will shower him with love rather than condemnation. When the son is still "a great way off," his father runs to greet and embrace him. His father does not remind him of his follies or hold a grudge but calls his family and servants to celebrate and rejoice together (Luke 15:20–24).

In our families, choosing mercy and forgiveness and extending love when our children have erred or have been corrected can establish the same loving environment in which family members know they are safe to learn and grow and still be loved. When we create homes full of love, our own prodigal children can know they can return to open arms despite the pain of their learning experiences.

Extending love when children err helps them feel safe and can create a desire to reform. Children need to know they will be loved no matter what mistakes they make or sins they commit. When true doctrine is taught and understood and love is felt, an ideal environment for self-propelled repentance is created. Correcting children is an integral part of helping them grow. Flooding that correction with encouragement and unconditional love helps growth happen in an optimal way. Tell your children you love them and know they can and will do better. Help them to see the potential you see in them. Trust your child to God's care. Know that He will help lead them with the timing and experiences that are best for them.

When Forgiving Is Hard

While considering such warming examples of love and forgiveness, it is important to note that sometimes family members cause true anguish for each other. Sometimes choices are devastating and forgiveness doesn't come quickly or easily. Many people are hurt deeply at some point in life by a family member, whether it is a parent, sibling, spouse, child, or other relative. If you fit into this category, please don't feel alone and blame others' actions on yourself. In these instances forgiveness can be a long, agonizing process.

At one point in my life I had been deeply hurt repeatedly over a period of years by a close family member. I felt I had forgiven past wrongs, but when fresh grievances arose, I again faced feelings of anger, betrayal, hurt, and loneliness. I wondered how to forgive this person once again. Over a period of months I prayed for peace, relief, and the strength to forgive. The forgiveness I was seeking didn't come quickly, but the Spirit did whisper that the Lord understood my pain. He knew my heart, that I wanted to forgive, and that I was hurting deeply. He did not condemn me for my inability to quickly forgive. He was patient with me while I processed raw feelings on my way to greater peace.

When I have been deeply hurt by the choices of loved ones, it has been helpful for me to eventually reach a point in my journey when I could consider the heart and life of the person who has hurt me. People who hurt others are almost always hurting themselves. When I consider the lives of those who have hurt me the most deeply, I recognize that they carry their own pain from their own past experiences. Recognizing the pain of an offender doesn't make their actions okay. But despite how hurtful some of their actions have been, I could see that they were each doing the best they could while managing their own problems and experiences. This does not take away my pain, but it does ease the forgiveness process a little. Some people who have suffered neglect, abuse, grief, or trauma hurt others without realizing it simply because they are hurting so much themselves. Often they are in too much pain to pause and consider how their actions affect others. Sometimes people who are haunted by their own painful pasts hurt others on purpose. But, deep inside, each one of us—the offended and the offenders—all long for love, peace, and healing.

Just as forgiveness of serious sins can require a process of time, drawing on Christ for strength to forgive and heal may also take time. Often the Lord lets us sort through feelings and experience hurt before taking the pain away. Sometimes it is in these deep, agonizing times that we come to know Christ and appreciate Him better. A loving, merciful Father had to require the Son to pass through the hardships of Gethsemane and Calvary. Our Savior's suffering in these experiences was because of the choices of others—us. The same Father and Son allow us our own smaller Gethsemane moments during which we wrestle, agonize, and cry out for relief, sometimes because of the choices of others. There aren't quick answers and relief in these times.

The good news is that in the end of these soul-stretching experiences we may find vibrant beauty as we realize what we have become through the process—more sure witnesses of Christ's divinity and Atonement, with deeper abilities to comprehend joy. Jesus Christ came to "heal the brokenhearted" (Luke 4:18). As we cry out to the Savior for healing and peace, over the course of time we change. The Spirit can whisper truth to teach us and make us whole. We can become more compassionate, loving, kind, and holy. Jesus Christ can ease the bitterness and fill us with His peace and love. The process of becoming sanctified through the grace of Christ is a long journey. But in exchange for our efforts and heartaches, Christ offers us joy.

Alma's experience with repentance describes this principle of joy in proportion to our sorrow. When the angel came to Alma the Younger and commanded him to repent, Alma was "racked with eternal torment" and "harrowed up to the greatest degree" (Alma 36:12). For days he anguished over the life he had led and wished he could cease to exist. The thought of being in the presence of God was terrible. After suffering "inexpressible horror" (Alma 36:14) for three days and nights, he remembered what his father had taught him about Jesus Christ, and he cried out to his Savior for mercy (see Alma 36:16–18). When he did he was filled with "joy as exceeding as was [his] pain" (Alma 36:20). In his repentance process Alma waded through great depths of horror and anguish as he realized the gravity of his sins. But when he called on the name of Jesus Christ, the joy that filled his soul was equal in magnitude to the pain he had felt. When a merciful Father and Savior allow us to suffer, they are allowing our souls to be carved into larger receptacles for joy—joy in proportion to the pain we have felt.

I have felt the healing power of the Savior in my own life as I have sought to replace feelings of hurt and anger with peace and love. I can testify that the Atonement of Jesus Christ is a real source of healing, hope, and joy. If you or a loved one are wading through your own Gethsemane moments, when pain is intense and forgiveness is hard to find, hang in there. Your Heavenly Father has a plan for you, with a beautiful ending. Trust in His hand. Seek for the peace and healing that come alone from our Savior Jesus Christ.

Finally remember that forgiveness is not a license for abuse. Have the courage to seek professional help, if necessary, and follow the Lord's guidance on your individual path to wholeness and joy. With the Spirit as a guide, some people need to prayerfully consider healthy boundaries to establish between themselves and an offender. These are individual matters in which the Lord can lead you to peace and healing as you follow His Spirit.

A Gift We Give

In the end, whether the road to forgiveness is quick and paved or arduous and bumpy, realize that forgiveness of others is a gift you give yourself. Sometimes others aren't affected by our willingness to forgive or our decision to hold a grudge. But when we forgive, we feel greater peace.

One year for Christmas when I was growing up, I wanted a specific doll. I knew she was expensive, and I wasn't sure I would ever get her. But on Christmas morning that year she became mine, and I cherished her throughout my childhood. Years flew by, and when my children were small, my mom sent my old doll to me. She was still in good shape, and occasionally my girls would play with her.

One day some friends came over to play, and when they left, my children and I started cleaning up all the toys that had been left out. While we were cleaning, I found my old doll—covered in permanent black marker that the visiting two-year-old had somehow found. I didn't know how I could ever repair the damage that had been done.

My oldest daughter was five at the time. She looked at the doll, looked at me, and asked, "Are you mad?"

"No," I replied. "That would be a waste of my energy."

And instantly I realized how true that statement was. Sometimes when we have been hurt deeply, anger is a natural response. But when we work to forgive, we feel peace, light, and joy. The Spirit of the Lord can reign in our hearts and homes. When we choose anger and judgment, we feel agitation and darkness—and it can suck away energy, love, and peace. Forgiveness is a gift we give ourselves, our families, and others.

Choosing to fill our homes with love and forgiveness isn't always easy. When the pain caused by a loved one is especially deep, forgiveness may be a long, hard process instead of a quick, simple choice. But as we make conscious choices to extend mercy, choose a soft answer, reprove gently, and fill our children with love, our homes can be havens of peace and joy.

Application

1. When you feel upset, step back and choose a constructive activity to help you calm down.
2. Try the President McKay approach—when you feel angry, bite your tongue and take a few minutes to calm down.
3. When your children err, stop to consider if it is a sin or a mistake. What doctrine or principle might you help them understand better to prevent further missteps?
4. Set a goal not to choose anger. Make this a matter of consistent prayer. Consider what you will do in specific situations instead of choosing anger. Role play possibilities with your spouse or a trusted friend.
5. When you feel like yelling, choose to lower your voice or whisper instead.

CHAPTER 6
Respect

"The most important setting to forgo contention and practice respect for differences is in our homes and family relationships." —Dallin H. Oaks[1]

RESPECT IS A VIRTUE THAT is sadly lacking in our world today. Too often the public arena is full of taunts, jeers, ridicule, name-calling, and condemnation. From bumper stickers to headlines we are bombarded with a societal culture of rudeness and vulgarity. Unfortunately, as respect has lessened in public, it has also deteriorated in homes and families. Parents and children are constantly surrounded by worldly examples of those who are openly disrespectful of others' feelings and needs. If we want our family members to be friends throughout the eternities, we must choose differently.

Establishing homes with respect requires constant vigilance and training. Admittedly this is difficult. Parenting tries the patience of the most virtuous people, and it is easy to slip and set an example that is less than kind, lovely, or respectful. Parents must pray, work, and apologize when necessary. Families should openly discuss standards for respectful language, actions, and communication, working to create a family culture of respect.

Respectful Language
Courtesy

One of the first areas to watch for respect is in our voices—both the things we say and how we say them. How often do family members demonstrate courtesy, saying please, thank you, and excuse me? The example of respect must come first from the parents; it is hard for children to rise above the standard they are shown. I think the following example from President Brigham Young

---

1 Dallin H. Oaks, "Loving Others and Living with Differences," *Ensign*, Nov. 2014, 27.

is instructive. He said, "How often we see parents demand obedience, good behavior, kind words, pleasant looks, a sweet voice and a bright eye from a child or children when they themselves are full of bitterness and scolding!"[2] Seasoned parents recognize that when they are sharp or impatient, an epidemic can quickly start among their children. If my children are harsh with each other, I have to respond with kindness and love, or things will only deteriorate from there. Parents must choose courteous, respectful language before they can rightfully expect it from their children.

Respectful language in a family requires modeling and constant training. Pay attention to how you talk to your children. How often do you show courtesy, and how often does impatience rule? Families are naturally busy and demanding, and it can be hard to maintain courtesy. However, a parental example of frequently saying please and thank you will go a long way to establish authority and respect in a home.

One way to monitor courtesy is to keep a log for a few days. Jot notes down on your phone, in a notebook, or on a computer every time you have a significant interaction with your children. Take note of what you ask or discuss and how you do it. Log how your children respond. Although logging takes a bit of extra time and effort, a quick review after a day or two establishes a clear picture. This will help you establish a baseline to know how your family is doing and where you can improve. I highly recommend keeping such a log for a day or two whenever family life seems contentious or off-kilter. Logging interactions and analyzing what really happens can clearly illustrate actions or principles that need more parental emphasis.

Kindness

In addition to choosing and teaching courtesy, it is wise to set an example of kindness and giving others the benefit of the doubt. When children are raised with criticism, they may learn to criticize. If they are shown forbearance, they have a greater chance of extending it to others. No one feels good if they are demeaned or ridiculed. Some families find it helpful to discuss and establish a family standard in this regard. If everyone agrees to not refer to themselves or others in insulting ways, everyone will feel better. If someone slips, gently remind them of the family standard until good habits are formed.

I love the story told by Marjorie Hinckley about her young granddaughter. After playing with a friend the granddaughter returned home feeling upset about something her friend said. When her mother asked what the friend

---

2 *Teachings of Presidents of the Church: Brigham Young* (1997), 173.

said, she replied, "Well, it's such a bad word that I can't say it, but it was 'shut [point upward]!'"[3] Wouldn't it be a glorious world if people didn't say *shut up* or other harsh words? I would love it if my children thought such phrases were so taboo. Unfortunately, in our world today, coarse language is everywhere. Despite what your children will hear from their peers and through media, you can set standards of what is acceptable in your home. Everyone will feel better if they choose respect.

President David O. McKay referred to "backbiting, evil-speaking, [and] faultfinding" as "destructive termites of homes." He taught, "In the ideal home, there is no slanderous gossip about . . . schoolteachers, about public officials, or Church officials. I am more grateful now, as years have come and gone, to my father, who with hands lifted said, 'Now, no faultfinding about your teacher or anybody else.'"[4] I love the example of that father who taught his children that criticizing others wasn't okay. Children feel safe in homes where parents consciously extend kindness and mercy to each other, to their children, and to others.

What does the kindness meter look like in your home? Are there steps you can take to cut back on criticizing, name-calling, or other harsh words?

Tone of Voice

While monitoring our word choice, it is also good to watch tone of voice. Raised voices, sarcasm, or harsh or impatient tones hurt feelings and destroy family harmony. Some families designate a key word to use as a signal when someone has said something unkind. The signal word in our home is "rewind." If someone uses harsh words or tone of voice, they are asked to rewind and try to say it again in a nicer way. Sometimes we ask our kids to rewind, and sometimes they ask us. Rewinding provides a valuable opportunity for people to recognize an error and fix it before harsh words and hurt feelings accumulate.

When respectful language becomes the standard in a home, hearts can remain open and communication can flow more freely. Choosing communication that is respectful, honest, open, and kind creates an atmosphere for loving relationships to grow.

Respecting Feelings

Maintaining respectful language at home requires constant monitoring and work. Another facet of respect that goes hand-in-hand with respectful

---

3 *Glimpses into the Life and Heart of Marjorie Pay Hinckley,* ed. Virginia H. Pearce (1999), 53.
4 *Teachings of Presidents of the Church: David O. McKay* (2003), 43.

language is respecting the feelings of other family members. This is tricky ground. Even when language is kind and courteous, families are full of people with individual experiences, needs, and feelings, and dealing with all of them can be overwhelming.

Respect for the feelings of others must start with the realization that everyone has feelings, and everyone's feelings are real to them. Children should learn that their feelings will be recognized and considered. I like the story shared by the Hinckleys about an extended family sightseeing trip around the Boston area. It was a hot day, and a two-year-old grandchild kept stripping down to his diaper to feel more comfortable. After two or three attempts to dress him only to have him quickly undress again, President Hinckley's wife giggled and said, "It's just too hot for clothes." The happy toddler spent his day sightseeing in his diaper.[5]

Many of us in a similar circumstance might have worried more about what people were thinking of our parenting choices. In this instance, Sister Hinckley was wise enough to recognize a battle that wasn't worth fighting. She respected the needs and feelings her grandson demonstrated and let him be.

Of course, parents should not give in to every tantrum and whim and let their toddlers (or teenagers) rule the world. Children can and should be expected to do things that are challenging and uncomfortable, despite whining and protests. Rules and boundaries are an essential part of raising happy youth, despite what your child may say to the contrary. We must be wise. Pause to consider your child's feelings and concerns and analyze your reasoning or fears. When a child is having a temper tantrum, choose to respond with love. Deep inside a storming child is a need for love and boundaries. I have found that if I hug, snuggle, or rub the back of a child who is having a meltdown, they may calm down more quickly. Other times children want space to sort out their feelings and experiences. Showing compassion for children's feelings does not mean I need to give them what they are ranting about; it simply means I want them to feel loved and supported while they sort out their feelings. After they are calm we can discuss any concerns and make sure they understand the situation appropriately.

When a child shares an experience or feeling, most of us instinctively respond by thinking about our own perceptions, feelings, or concerns. Instead of telling your child what she should do or say, begin by asking questions or recognizing feelings. You could say, "You are feeling sad because . . ." Thinking about your child's experiences and feelings shows that she can trust you to

---

5 *Glimpses into the Life and Heart of Marjorie Pay Hinckley,* ed. Virginia H. Pearce (1999), 56.

keep sharing more. Respecting her feelings demonstrates love and designates your relationship as a safe place for sharing experiences.

Children go through stages, and sometimes those stages are taxing for parents. Remembering that your child's needs and stages will change is helpful to keep a healthy perspective. Listen to your children. Consider their viewpoints and their experiences. As hard as it is to endure through some phases, how you do it may contribute to how quickly and gracefully your child graduates from that phase.

Sometimes as parents we feel like stomping our feet, drawing a figurative line in the sand, and announcing that our child has got to change and we cannot handle one more day of the status quo. Proceed with caution when you feel that way, and keep a doctrinal perspective. Is your child's behavior signaling a lack of training or a need? Is there something you can teach a bit better? Do they have a deep need that is being expressed, however taxing it may feel to you as their parent? Is there something they are trying to sort out inside themselves? Might patience (as hard as it is) still be the better course?

Preserving Your Relationship

I have often pondered a key phrase Marjorie Hinckley taught her daughter-in-law. When the daughter-in-law was a young mother, she would call Sister Hinckley for counsel on a variety of parenting dilemmas. Did she need to go to extreme lengths to rescue a child from disappointment? When should her children take swimming lessons? When all the neighboring mothers "were tossing their reluctant, screaming children into the teacher's outstretched arms in the pool," she wondered if she shouldn't do the same. Her child needed to learn to swim sometime, right? Sister Hinckley gave advice that her daughter-in-law would say "over and over to [herself] for many years to come, 'Just save the relationship.'" Sister Hinckley's daughter-in-law concluded, "I believe those words are the most simple and powerful parenting principle I have ever learned."[6]

Some of the battles we pick with our children aren't really necessary. All children go through difficult stages. All people have quirks that require patience and love from others. If you recognize that your child's feelings and needs are real, you can focus on saving the relationship with your child, respect her individuality, and allow her to grow. When you do, both of you will feel better. When a child's needs are exhausting and it is tempting to choose an arbitrary deadline for her progress, consider her feelings and long-term needs.

6 *Glimpses into the Life and Heart of Marjorie Pay Hinckley,* ed. Virginia H. Pearce (1999), 55–56.

If you choose gentle encouragement and love, your child can maintain trust that she can depend on you to guide and help her.

Sometimes when I feel frustrated with a child's slow progress, it is helpful to think of the example set by our Savior. Thankfully, He never throws His hands in the air and declares that He has been patient with us long enough and if we don't figure out perfection by the end of the year, we will be left on our own. No, Christ sets an example of patience, long-suffering, and love. If we are to maintain the trust and respect of our children, we must do the same.

Respectful Discipline

Parenting can be demanding and exhausting, and sometimes parents don't know how to help a child through a struggle or behavior problem. As parental frustration rises, it is easy to think in terms of what you will do to your child if things don't change. However, in addition to respectful language and respect for feelings, respectful discipline is essential to creating a loving home and maintaining loving relationships.

Loving and Leading

President Russell M. Nelson told of a time when he came home from work as a young father to find his wife exhausted from a day of mothering duties. Trying to help out, he began ordering his daughters to get ready for bed in a manner "befitting the demeanor of a drill sergeant." One young daughter approached him and thoughtfully asked, "Daddy, do you own me?" He quickly realized that his demands were closer to unrighteous dominion than to the Savior's example of patience and love. He later taught, "We don't own our children; we have them for a short season. As parents, we have the privilege to love them, to lead them, and then to let them go."[7]

I think those are key points for parents choosing discipline methods. We don't own our children, and we owe them the same respect and courtesy we would show a friend or stranger. We must choose discipline that leads children and demonstrates love. Let's explore these concepts.

President Gordon B. Hinckley taught, "There is no discipline in all the world like the discipline of love. It has a magic all its own."[8] It is wise to step back at times and think about your choices as a parent. What are the true motives behind your actions? It is easy to assign consequences out of sheer exhaustion and frustration, motivated more by revenge than by love. However, children are keen observers, and if love is not truly your motivation in a given circumstance, they will probably pick up on it.

---

7 Spencer J. Condie, *Russell M. Nelson: Father, Surgeon, Apostle* (2003), 79.
8 *Teachings of Presidents of the Church: Gordon B. Hinckley* (2016), 174.

The root word of discipline is disciple—to be a follower. Our actions as parents should teach and lift and set an example for our children to follow. President Brigham Young taught, "I do not believe in making my authority as a husband or a father known by brute force; but by a superior intelligence—by showing them that I am capable of teaching them."[9] Good discipline teaches a child proper behavior in a persuasive, gentle, loving way rather than a forceful or overpowering way.

If children are misbehaving, consider the message behind their actions. What might they need to understand? What need are they expressing? What would be an uplifting way of teaching them? Michaelene Grassli, former Primary general president, taught, "While we need to help children learn to control behaviors that are not constructive, it is helpful to remember that those actions are not necessarily misbehavior. And when children do misbehave, they usually do so not because they intend to be naughty, but because they are being the best they can be for their age."[10]

Making a child feel bad through harsh means—yelling, scolding, applying negative labels, or hitting—doesn't inspire him to do better; often such actions create resentment and discouragement. Both children and adults respond better when they are encouraged and loved rather than criticized and demeaned.

Parenting experiences try the patience and resolve of the most saintly people, and choosing disciplinary methods that teach and set an example for children takes practice and persistence. Punitive means of discipline teach children fear, but they can seem tempting because they appear to produce immediate results. However, Elder Dieter F. Uchtdorf has taught that "fear rarely has the power to change our hearts, and it will never transform us into people who love what is right and who want to obey Heavenly Father. People who are fearful may *say* and do the right things, but they do not *feel* the right things."[11] Avoiding such tactics requires stamina as parents thoroughly teach and reteach children essential lessons. In the end, showing respect for your children in the ways you teach them allows love and respect to grow. Let me share an example from our home.

It was a few weeks before Christmas, our house was feeling cluttered and messy, and I was dreading the onslaught of new toys and gadgets that is often synonymous with the holiday season. As I went through my day, I noticed countless examples of sloppiness—family members hadn't put things away properly or had performed their jobs carelessly. My frustration mounted as the

9 *Teachings of Presidents of the Church: Brigham Young* (1997), 339.
10 Michaelene P. Grassli, "Teaching Our Children," *Ensign*, April 1994, 62.
11 Dieter F. Uchtdorf, "Perfect Love Casteth Out Fear," *Ensign*, May 2017, 105, emphases in original.

hours passed, and internally I seethed and dreamed of punitive measures to motivate change. That night as I knelt to pray, I poured out my frustration to the Lord and asked for His thoughts on how I should proceed. The inspiration that came was that I needed to put more emphasis on exactness as I dealt with our children (see Alma 57:21). The next month we instigated a weekly family award for exactness that we would give to a child who had performed tasks precisely. When asking children to put something away or correcting something that had been done sloppily, I would remind the children to do their jobs with exactness. In family council we discussed examples of exactness and worked to raise our children's awareness of that virtue. Of course, this solution did not bring a quick resolution, but it did provide ample means for me to properly teach my children. It was consistent and instructive rather than discouraging or demeaning. President Russell M. Nelson has taught, "When a child needs correction, you might ask yourself, 'What can I say or do that would persuade him or her to choose a better way?' . . . To be persuasive, your love must be sincere and your teachings based on divine doctrine and correct principles."[12] Disciplining with love, patience, and doctrine is sometimes different from what the world advocates, but it is a godly way of teaching children the correct way to behave.

Training Children to Think

When your children need to be disciplined, consider how you can teach them in a loving, encouraging way. Children need to receive the message that everyone makes mistakes and you know they can and will do better. Teach them how to think through situations they didn't handle well. This can be managed in a few different ways. One is to privately sit down and discuss a scenario in which your child's behavior was undesirable. Help the child consider possible reactions and what she should do differently. A second option would be to ask your child to write down the situation, along with her possible responses and the advantages and disadvantages of each response. This exercise encourages children to thoroughly consider a scenario and what the best response might be. Finally, parents can role play a situation with a child. If the situation involves multiple siblings, role play it with them all together. These methods allow your children to think through their options and consider what they could do differently. They instill hope and confidence that your children can improve.

Let me share an example of how one of these methods can work. If one of my children is having a hard time responding appropriately in a situation, I might sit down with him to complete a SODAS—a popular problem-solving technique

12 Russell M. Nelson, "Salvation and Exaltation," *Ensign*, May 2008, 9–10.

advocated in parenting or conflict-resolution circles.[13] SODAS is an acronym: Situation, Options, Disadvantages, Advantages, Solution. The first step is to clearly outline the situation that is causing concern. The second step is to list all possible options the child is faced with in that specific situation. In the third step, the child will list all the disadvantages of each option they listed in step two. In the fourth step, the child will list the advantages of each option listed. The fifth step is for the child to choose which of all the options outlined is the best one.

If a child is old enough to write, I would expect her to jot down her answers. If she cannot write, I might sit down to talk with her about everything and write down her responses for her. Here is one possible example:

Situation	Options	Disadvantages	Advantages	Solution
I am asked to complete a chore.	I can disobey and go play.	I will still be expected to do the job later when I am caught, along with additional work so I can practice being obedient.	I get to go play right away.	Do my chore when I'm asked.
	I can do the job.	I have to do the job.	I can be done quicker and can play afterward.	

In addition to using SODAS to help our children rethink their actions, we also might assign a SODAS if a child's attitude needs to improve. Here is one possible example:

Situation	Options	Disadvantages	Advantages	Solution
I lose when we play a board game.	I can choose to congratulate the winner.	I need enough self-control to tell the winner "Good job."	Everyone feels better, including me.	Choose to be a gracious player.
	I can pout and claim I should have won.	I feel grumpy, and I have to write a SODAS.	I get to vent my feelings.	

We have found that the SODAS method is an excellent technique for teaching our children to think about their choices and choose the best response in a variety of daily frustrations as well as individual concerning scenarios. I like to keep a typed sheet handy in our home, with each step clearly outlined. When my children need to think through their responses a little better, I hand them a sheet and ask them to start writing.

13 For more information about the SODAS method, visit http://www.tipstars.org/ Portals/0/pdf/Mod5-SODAS.pdf.

Children need boundaries and consequences. Elder Jeffrey R. Holland instructed parents, "Second only to your love, [your children] need your limits."[14] Wise parents set an example of love and discipline and administer consequences that are respectful, logical, instructive, and encouraging. If a child makes a mess or breaks something, expect him to clean it, pay for it, or make restitution. This system can start with toddlers. If your two-year-old decorates your wall with crayons or markers, calmly and cheerfully sit down with your child and a couple of rags and clean it together. This method teaches your child proper behavior and allows her to correct her mistake. Making things right feels good.

Good discipline requires a bit of creativity. Remember that your job is to teach your children to think well and act appropriately. What will help them do that? Is your child's attitude detrimental? Ask him to compile a list of twenty things he is grateful for or help him start keeping a gratitude journal. Does one of your children have a hard time being nice to another sibling? Ask her to write a short paper listing that sibling's talents and strengths. On occasion we have chosen the traditional assignment of asking a child to copy a specific sentence such as *I will be obedient, My job is to love my siblings*, or *I will treat others with respect* ten times. Sometimes it is helpful to present your concern to your child, discuss the situation, and ask your child to suggest a solution. Given an opportunity couched in love, children can often think of circumstances that will help them choose better. And when they have thought of the solution, they may be more receptive to learning from it.

Some parents choose to temporarily withdraw a privilege as a way of teaching their child. There is divine precedent for this choice: Joseph Smith's possession of the gold plates and his ability to translate them were temporarily removed after the loss of the 116 pages. Of this experience Elder Lynn G. Robbins explained, "Because the Lord wanted to teach Joseph a heart-changing lesson, He required a heartrending sacrifice of him—sacrifice being an essential part of discipline."[15] It is important to note how the Lord encouraged Joseph through this experience. When the plates were taken, the Lord told Joseph, "Behold, thou art Joseph, and thou wast chosen to do the work of the Lord, but because of transgression, if thou art not aware thou wilt fall. But remember, God is merciful; therefore, repent of that which thou hast done which is contrary to the commandment which I gave you, and thou art still chosen, and art again called to the work" (D&C 3:9–10). The Lord offered Joseph hope, encouragement, and instruction through this experience.

14 Jeffrey R. Holland, "To Young Women," *Ensign*, Nov. 2005, 29.
15 Lynn G. Robbins, "The Righteous Judge," *Ensign*, Nov. 2016, 97.

If your children could benefit from a temporary loss of privileges, emphasize your love, expectations, and confidence in their ability to make better choices. Don't apply consequences for long periods of time that might discourage children or make them feel like they can't repent. Remember, your motivation must be love, not vengeance, and you want your child to feel hope and encouragement. Sometimes a simple time-out to let a child reset is most effective. Time-outs don't have to be punitive. A child can be encouraged to read or choose another quiet activity to help them change their current actions and mindset. Sometimes sitting with young children and participating in a constructive activity together can help a child do better. Other times, a chore might help. Hard work is productive and feels good. Handled correctly and lovingly by the parent, all of these sacrifices required of children—time, energy, or privileges—can teach children about correct behavior and help them experience a change of heart.

Effective discipline often requires parents to step back and consciously think about what they want to teach and how to do it. Sometimes this means doing things differently from how they were raised. If this is the case for you, recognize that one of the best ways you can honor your parents is to raise your children with love and respect. Peace comes as we accept that our parents did the best they could in their own circumstances. Pray deeply, listen to your heart, and raise your children the way the Spirit prompts you. Recognize that good discipline also requires you to consider each child individually. What will work best for one child might not be the answer for another, because each child is unique. Pray for guidance over each specific situation you need help with. Rely on the Lord to lead you in your journey of raising righteous children.

Parenting children isn't a quick task—it takes eternal love and work. Sometimes parents feel tempted by punitive means that seem to offer quick fixes. It is wise to remember that the real goals of parenting are loving and teaching. When teaching is done in a loving, encouraging way, children will feel better, respond better, and live better. When parents discipline their children respectfully, they send a clear message of hope, encouragement, and love.

Offering Trust and Respecting Agency

Another important way parents respect their children is through demonstrating trust and allowing children to use their own agency. The Prophet Joseph Smith's famous words are appropriate parenting counsel: a parent's end goal should be to "teach [their children] correct principles, and [let them] govern themselves."[16]

---

16 *Teachings of Presidents of the Church: Joseph Smith* (2007), 284.

President George Albert Smith recalled his mother's gentle counsel for him to not play ball with the neighborhood boys on a Sunday. "She did not say, 'You cannot do it,' but she did say: 'Son, you will be happier if you do not do that.'" He said, "I want to tell you I am grateful for that kind of training in the home."[17]

President Heber J. Grant chose a similar course in raising his children. His daughter recalled that, in small matters, her father rarely said no so that the children would know how seriously he meant it when a no was required. Whenever possible, he would explain his thoughts and then say, "That's the way I feel about it; but of course, you must decide for yourself." His relaxed manner made it easier for his children to want to choose correctly without feeling compelled.[18]

Marjorie Hinckley's philosophy was "never to say 'no' if [she] could possibly say 'yes.'" She felt that "gave [her] children the feeling that [she] trusted them and they were responsible to do the best they could."[19] Children may feel more loved and confident and may be more likely to rise to the occasion when they are trusted and allowed to choose.

Enlarging the boundaries around a child's behavior and introducing increased use of agency is a gradual process. Obviously young children cannot be allowed to choose whether they want to use their seat belts, for example. As children grow and have received proper instruction and boundaries, express confidence as you allow them to make appropriate choices in their lives. Make sure your child understands the situation and potential consequences. Don't soften consequences or abdicate parental responsibility to properly teach and prepare your children for life's lessons.

Deciding when you should enlarge a boundary and allow a child to make a choice and learn from its consequences is a very individual matter that must be made through prayer and inspiration. Should you let your child decide what to do about a questionable party invitation? Should a contrary child be allowed to choose whether or not to attend church? What boundaries should you place on your child's media choices? These are delicate matters best decided with divine help. Counsel with your spouse, if you are married, and with your child. Teach doctrine. Pray for guidance and inspiration. Encourage your children to be prayerful about their choices. In these moments it is easy for parents to be pulled into cycles of fear, worrying about potential outcomes and future problems. But the best way to work with your child is through love, faith, and trust.

---

17 *Teachings of Presidents of the Church: George Albert Smith* (2011), 169.

18 *Teachings of Presidents of the Church: Heber J. Grant* (2002), 200.

19 *Glimpses into the Life and Heart of Marjorie Pay Hinckley,* ed. Virginia H. Pearce (1999), 55.

Respecting children's agency and trusting children does not ensure they will always make flawless choices. President Spencer W. Kimball was once questioned about allowing his children to play table tennis on a Sunday. He responded, "I don't do it, but they must decide for themselves."[20] Learning from mistakes and finding appropriate ways to exercise agency is the process of a lifetime for all of us. Often parents want to shelter their children from incorrect choices and their consequences. Elder Larry Y. Wilson of the Seventy taught, "Wise parents prepare their children to get along without them. They provide opportunities for growth as children acquire the spiritual maturity to exercise their agency properly. And yes, this means children will sometimes make mistakes and learn from them."[21] Allowing children to exercise the agency Heavenly Father already gave them lets them build inner faith and character as they make their own discoveries. Parents must be careful not to rescue children from the consequences of their choices and thereby prevent them from learning essential lessons.

Trust Fosters Love

One of the first steps parents must take when respecting agency is to demonstrate love. When children feel loved they will be more likely to listen to a parent's counsel. If children recognize a mistake, they will be less afraid to share their learning experience with parents. Love keeps families united. Parents who demonstrate love by trusting their children help keep communication lines open and make it easier for children to feel loved and empowered.

An experience shared by Elder Larry Y. Wilson demonstrates respecting a child's agency while extending love and teaching correct doctrine. When his daughter Mary's soccer team made it to the championships, the big game was scheduled for a Sunday. Mary had been taught the value of the Sabbath throughout her youth. Her parents read scriptures with her and encouraged her to pray about her decision. Perhaps responding to pressure from her coach and team, she chose to play in the game. Her parents discussed the choice with her, prayed, and allowed her to carry out her decision.

After the championship game, Mary walked over to her mother and said, "That felt awful. I never want to feel that way again. I'm never playing another game on the Sabbath day."[22]

---

20 Caroline Eyring Miner and Edward L. Kimball, *Camilla: A Biography of Camilla Eyring Kimball* (1980), 110.

21 Larry Y. Wilson, "Only upon the Principles of Righteousness," *Ensign*, May 2012, 104.

22 Wilson, "Only upon the Principles of Righteousness," 104–105.

Mary's parents had taught her throughout her life and read scriptures with her to aid in her decision-making process. They allowed her to choose, and that became a powerful learning experience. If her parents had chosen for her, stepped back in the teaching process, or withheld love, she might have had a harder time learning from her choices.

The Savior taught that if we want to know if the gospel is true, we must make choices to try it and find out for ourselves (see John 7:17). Our Father in Heaven recognizes that true learning comes from experience. If parents deny their children the opportunity to make their own choices, their children can't become truly converted.

Sometimes parents watch their children use agency in ways that are terrifying. Sometimes there don't appear to be any golden learning moments from which children quickly recognize the error of their ways. Be patient, faithful, and prayerful. Your responsibility as a parent is not to make all your children's choices for them. God gave them their agency just as He gave you yours. Neither is it your responsibility to save your children from their choices. Jesus Christ already paid the price to be your child's Savior. Remember that wise parents seek to draw nearer to Christ, teach their children appropriately, and set an example for their children to follow. President Russell M. Nelson taught, "As we go through life . . . a [parent's] instinctive impulse to cling tightly . . . to his children may not be the best way to accomplish his objective. Instead, if he will lovingly cling to the Savior and the iron rod of the gospel, his family will want to cling to him and to the Savior."[23] Love your children, and express your trust and confidence in them. Teach them truth in ways that will help it sink into their souls. As they are old enough and are properly taught and prepared, step back and respect their choices. Allow them to make mistakes, and when they do, express love, compassion, and empathy. Pray mightily, trust your Savior and Heavenly Father, and trust your children to learn from their experiences.

Building a Family Culture of Respect

With essential elements of respectful language and discipline and respect for feelings and agency in place, families lay a foundation for building a family culture of respect. However, if families want to maximize the synergy that can occur from a united family unit, they must learn to regularly listen to each other and counsel together.

---

23 Spencer J. Condie, *Russell M. Nelson: Father, Surgeon, Apostle* (2003), 97.

Listening to Understand

As simple as it sounds, truly listening and understanding each other often gets lost in the crush of schedules, needs, and concerns. Do your children feel like you understand their feelings, experiences, and challenges? How often do you look into each child's eyes and share thoughts in open, respectful ways?

Often when we converse with other people, we are thinking more about our point of view and our feelings than about the other person's experiences and feelings. Sometimes it helps to stop and focus on the other person, exploring and validating their feelings. Cameron and I have found that a dialogue process[24] designed to help couples communicate effectively works well with our children as well. We posted a paper by our kitchen table with the following dialogue suggestions:

Situation	Options
"I want to talk about something."	"Okay," or suggest an appropriate time.
"I feel . . ." Explain what happened and how you feel.	"So you . . ." Restate Person A's feelings as you understand them and then say, "Is that right?"
Continue stating and explaining feelings as necessary.	"That makes sense because . . ." Validate Person A's feelings.
Acknowledge and explain.	When Person A feels ready, switch roles and explain anything you need to.

When our kids had a major disagreement, we would sit them down at the kitchen table and encourage them to use these skills to really listen to each other. Although these suggestions may sound basic, they can be difficult to implement when emotions are high. But when used well, such effective listening skills sometimes allow tender feelings to come out, and it is an opportunity for everyone to understand each other better.

As a parent, when I practice really listening to and validating my children's feelings, I am given a deeper view into their experiences and concerns as I teach them that I care about understanding them. Listening to understand teaches family members to think about how others feel and to understand how their own actions affect others. Instead of jumping in to insert a solution or countering viewpoint, you allow your children to fully share their hearts. When parents model effective listening in their interactions with their children, family members can understand each other's hearts better and come away feeling understood.

---

24 Laura M. Brotherson, *And They Were Not Ashamed: Strengthening Marriage through Sexual Fulfillment* (2004), 199–200.

Family Council

Parents can also make great strides toward developing a family culture of listening and respect by holding a weekly family council meeting. Regular family councils give a chance for all family members to discuss matters and weigh in on decisions. President M. Russell Ballard taught that children "need a calm setting where discussion can take place on rules or principles they do not understand—a place where they know they are loved and at which their voice will at least be heard. Family councils are ideal forums for effective communication to take place. Family rules and procedures are more likely to be accepted and followed if all family members have been given the opportunity to participate in the discussions and agree to the rules."[25]

Family councils provide a wonderful way to discuss major decisions, such as finances and family vacations, as well as minor rules that need to be addressed or reviewed. When President Ezra Taft Benson and his wife were raising their family, they counseled on issues such as major financial expenditures and where to live.[26]

Elder Robert D. Hales of the Quorum of the Twelve Apostles recommended that families use family council as a regular time to address and discuss their budget, savings, and expenses. "This will teach our children to recognize the difference between wants and needs and to plan ahead for meaningful use of family resources,"[27] he said. Family council is a great place to regularly review how the family is doing with sections of the budget in which everyone's choices can contribute to success—items such as groceries or utilities. This habit introduces children to basic principles of budgeting and saving and helps everyone feel ownership in the family's financial successes.

Family councils are also a natural venue for additional teaching. In our family councils, we routinely role play and review manners, standards, expectations, and social graces. (If a parent is willing to really ham up some scenarios, this can be enjoyable for everyone.) Family councils are also where our family addresses chronic issues such as sloppiness or bickering between siblings. We can discuss as needed how to perform different jobs with exactness or role play how to respond appropriately if a sibling is irritating. When this is handled in an open, light way, offense can be kept at bay as everyone participates in a productive discussion or activity.

---

25 M. Russell Ballard, *Counseling with Our Councils: Learning to Minister Together in the Church and in the Family* (2012), 165.

26 Sheri L. Dew, *Ezra Taft Benson: A Biography* (Salt Lake City: Deseret Book, 1987), 150.

27 Robert D. Hales, "Becoming Provident Providers Temporally and Spiritually," *Ensign*, May 2009, 9.

Regular family councils build unity and establish a family culture of respect. Children learn that their feelings and opinions matter. President M. Russell Ballard has said that "too often family councils are held only when the parents feel there are problems—and when parents think they have all the answers. . . . Remember, although children never have the right to be disrespectful to their parents, they are entitled to be heard."[28] If family councils are only called when there is a crisis, or if they are used as a pulpit for parents to preach and condemn, no one will enjoy or benefit from the process.

President M. Russell Ballard has also taught that "a family council, when conducted with love and with Christlike attributes, will counter the impact of modern technology that often distracts us from spending quality time with each other and also tends to bring evil right into our homes." He further counseled that "electronic devices need to be turned off so everyone can look at and listen to each other. During family councils and at other appropriate times, you may want to have a basket for the electronic devices so when the family gathers, everyone—including Mom and Dad—can deposit his or her phones, tablets, and MP3 players in the basket."[29]

We started holding regular family councils when our two oldest children were ages three and one. Because we knew they wouldn't sit still and stay engaged for long, we decided that family councils in our home would be held around a big bowl of popcorn. Every Sunday evening our family gathers to munch popcorn and discuss family affairs.

After a prayer, we like to start family council by going around the circle and letting each family member contribute something positive. Some weeks we all say something we're grateful for or something we're looking forward to. Other weeks we go around the circle and say what we love about each other. These icebreakers start things on a light, happy note.

We keep an agenda for family council on a whiteboard in our kitchen, and anyone can contribute an agenda item throughout the week. If a child comes to me with a concern about something, I encourage them to write it on the whiteboard. We discuss calendar and planning items and review progress on family goals, and then we proceed with training and discussion. We have also found that it is helpful to keep light minutes of any decisions. Invariably in the coming weeks someone will say, "We talked about this in family council," and when that happens it's helpful to have resolutions written down.

Some weeks there isn't anything on our family council agenda. We still hold family council. If all we do is eat popcorn together, share what we're looking forward to that week, and discuss the family calendar, we still believe

28 M. Russell Ballard, *Counseling with Our Councils*, 164–65.
29 M. Russell Ballard, "Family Councils," *Ensign*, May 2016, 63.

firmly in the beauty of this tradition. Weekly family councils bring our family together in an important bonding session in which we can listen, learn, and celebrate togetherness.

We like to end our family councils on a light note, with awards, a family cheer, and a group hug. Family councils ensure that all family members are heard and involved, and they provide a wonderful sense of family unity.

President M. Russell Ballard has taught that "family councils have always been needed. They are, in fact, eternal."[30] Family councils teach children that they are valued, that their thoughts and feelings matter, and that each member is needed in the family unit. In family councils parents demonstrate that each person is respected and loved.

Family Executive Committee Meeting

In anticipation of family council, it is wise for parents to come prepared and united. Elder L. Tom Perry recommended a "family executive committee meeting to plan family strategy. The executive committee, composed of a husband and wife, would meet together to fully communicate, discuss, plan, and prepare for their leadership role in the family organization."[31] There is much for parents to plan and prepare for, but time quickly slips by if parents aren't vigilant. If you are married, arrange for a regular time to plan together with your spouse, perhaps as part of a weekly date, early on Sunday morning, or at another workable time. Keep a little notebook where either spouse can jot down discussion items.

A family executive committee meeting is a wonderful time to discuss each child and how they are doing. President M. Russell Ballard recommended that parents use the executive committee meeting to "review each child's physical, emotional, and spiritual needs and his or her progress."[32] Again, keep notes of decisions and goals. If your spouse is in charge of talking to a child about a specific concern or you agreed to be responsible for teaching a child a new skill, make note and follow through. How is your family culture doing with issues such as love, respect, integrity, and kindness? Are there additional steps you would like to take to train your family with critical issues such as budgeting, work, or responsibility? Parents who plan together can pray and work to carve out their long-term goals and vision for their family.

Most parents love their children deeply and sacrifice for them. But in the pressures of daily life, sometimes respect can get lost. Demonstrating respect

30 M. Russell Ballard, "Family Councils," *Ensign*, May 2016, 63.
31 As cited in M. Russell Ballard, *Counseling with Our Councils*, 157.
32 M. Russell Ballard, "Family Councils," 64.

for your child through appropriate voice, language, and discipline is essential to keeping communication open. Extending trust and letting children learn from personal experiences allows them to grow in an atmosphere where they don't fear condemnation. Practicing effective listening and holding regular family councils demonstrates respect for each family member and allows the family unit to thrive.

Application

1. How is the tone of language around your home? Consider choosing a signal key word to remind family members when they need to try again.

2. Keep a courtesy log for a few days. Note the ways you demonstrate courtesy toward your children and where there is room for improvement.

3. Choose to respect family members' feelings. If children throw temper tantrums, demonstrate love and concern. When they have calmed down, you can discuss concerns and help them understand the situation.

4. When disciplining a child, choose methods that love, lead, teach, and encourage. Consider role playing scenarios or helping your child compose a SODAS.

5. As much as possible, respect your children's agency and allow them to learn from their own choices. Exercising agency should always be prefaced by abundant teaching and surrounded on all sides by demonstrations of love.

6. Find a workable time to hold family council every week. Keep it pleasant and upbeat. Allow everyone to contribute to the agenda, and keep basic minutes of family decisions.

7. Hold consistent family executive committee meetings with your spouse. Counsel together about each child and any goals you might set to help them.

CHAPTER 7
Love

More can be accomplished for good by unfeigned love, in bringing up a child, than by any other influence. —Joseph F. Smith[1]

"To you who are parents, I say, show love to your children," taught President Thomas S. Monson. "You know you love them, but make certain they know it as well. They are so precious. Let them know."[2] Put so succinctly it sounds quite simple, doesn't it? However, in just a short time you will put this book back down and be faced with reality: dirty dishes, piles of laundry, arguing children, or any other array of stresses. With all the demands of family life piled on, showing love becomes harder. Often, helping children feel loved requires a bit of concentrated effort.

Parents can show their love in a variety of ways. Living the values expressed in this book, such as forgiveness and respect, demonstrates love for your children. When you go to work, clean your house, cook, pay bills, or ferry your children to their various activities, you are showing love, although they might not recognize that for several years. So parents must consciously and regularly demonstrate love for each of their children in a way their children will recognize.

Parents can make a few simple, conscious habits to provide a fertile seedbed for love to grow in their families. Verbally expressing love is an essential first step. Pause and consider how often you look your children in the eye and tell each individually how much you love them, what they mean to you, and how important they are to your family. Smile at them. Hug them tightly or snuggle with them. Laugh with them. If most of your children's interactions with

---

1 Francis M. Gibbons, *Joseph F. Smith: Patriarch and Preacher, Prophet of God* (1984), 289.

2 *Teachings of Thomas S. Monson*, comp. Lynne F. Cannegieter (2011), 211.

you are positive, they will receive the message that you love them and enjoy spending time with them. I can notice a difference in our home when I make a conscious effort to look at my children, smile at them, laugh with them, and give them individual attention. Discipline issues minimize, the overall tone of our home improves, and everyone feels better.

What are other choices that signal to each of your children that they are important to you? This chapter will explore ways to demonstrate love for children individually as well as ways to build more love in your family unit.

Praising and Encouraging

President Henry B. Eyring once watched his father talk to someone who was clearly not performing to his potential. Afterward he asked his father why he didn't "let that guy have it." His father's sage response was, "The world knocks them down. I try to build them up."[3] This is wonderful parenting counsel. Occasionally we feel like really letting our children have it. Often life knocks our children down enough already. What they need is parents who will build them up and believe in them—even when their behavior doesn't give parents much to believe in.

Truly the world knocks everyone down, and consequently the world is full of people who are craving a kind word of encouragement. Virginia H. Pearce, former member of the Young Women general presidency, told a story about a little boy who wanted his mother to play darts with him. Finally giving in to his pleading, she followed him down to the basement before confessing that she didn't know the rules or how to play. "'Oh, it's not hard at all,' he beamed confidently. 'I just stand right here and throw the darts, and you stand over there and say, 'Wonderful! Wonderful!'"[4] I love that story. All of us would deeply appreciate such a cheering section, wouldn't we? We as parents yearn for words of thanks and recognition from our children; in a similar way, our children long for us to recognize all their potential and encourage them in their daily lives.

Cultivating a habit of recognizing and mentioning your children's strengths will encourage them and help them feel loved. Sit down and compose a list of your children's strengths. Having a list to consider can give a parent a point of reference or help a parent who is discouraged and looking for something to praise. How often do you compliment your children on their

3 Henry J. Eyring, *Mormon Scientist: The Life and Faith of Henry Eyring* (2007), 278.

4 Virginia H. Pearce, "Ward and Branch Families: Part of Heavenly Father's Plan for Us," *Ensign*, Nov. 1993, 80.

worthy attributes? Elder Lynn G. Robbins said, "In helping children discover who they are and helping strengthen their self-worth, we can appropriately compliment their achievement or behavior—the *do*. But it would be even wiser to focus our primary praise on their character and beliefs—who they *are*."[5] Teaching your children who they are through focusing on their positive qualities is an incredible gift you can give!

On one occasion, Elder Neal A. Maxwell was uplifted through his mother's ability to recognize character and offer encouragement. Young Neal was trying to ride a pony. After being thrown several times, he gave up and watched while a younger boy tamed and rode the pony. Feeling disheartened and beat up physically and emotionally, he met his mother. She said, "I remember looking out of the window and seeing you bucked off. You were angry, but you gave him a hard look and took the bridle and led him back to the barn. You were always kind to the animals."[6] His mother emphasized his successes and strength of character in order to lift him back up.

What are your children's natural talents? How can you more frequently point out their character strengths to encourage and lift them up? If children hear a sentence or two from you praising and encouraging their positive attributes and efforts throughout each day, they may feel more loved and optimistic.

Encouragement Changes Behavior

In addition to demonstrating love, offering a compliment is a powerful way to alter behavior. President David O. McKay once taught his son that complimenting a person on something done right is "the best way of criticizing"; it can show a person that another behavior is less desirable while also helping them feel good about better choices.[7] This is absolutely true of children. It is so easy for parents to harp on little negative habits. Instead, shower your children with love and encouragement when they do something right.

President David O. McKay's wife, Emma Rae, had a meaningful experience in which she learned the power of praise to help someone change course. Before her marriage, she taught school for a year. On the first day of class the principal came into the room and publicly announced that Emma Rae should watch out for one particular boy. "He is the worst boy in school," the principal

5 Lynn G. Robbins, "What Manner of Men and Women Ought Ye to Be?" *Ensign*, May 2011, 105, emphases in original
6 Bruce C. Hafen, *A Disciple's Life: The Biography of Neal A. Maxwell* (2002), 74.
7 David Lawrence McKay, *My Father, David O. McKay* (1989), 164.

said. Wisely, Emma Rae wrote the boy a note that said, "I think the principal was mistaken about your being a bad boy. I trust you and know you are going to help me make this room the best in school." Subsequently the boy was one of the best-behaved students for the rest of the school year.[8]

If children feel like their parents don't believe in them or often disapprove of them or their choices, they will feel discouraged and may be more likely to misbehave. When they frequently receive messages that they are loved, recognized, and appreciated, they may be more likely to rise to the occasion. The challenge for us as parents is to hunt for the good, point it out, and show our children how lovable and capable they are.

When President Harold B. Lee was a young father, he worked to encourage his daughters by telling them they already were "whatever it was that he wanted [them] to become." So in turn, his daughters "didn't ever want him to find out that [they] weren't really as good as he thought [they] were. [They] always wanted him to be proud of [them]." Both of the Lee daughters were enrolled in music lessons, and their father told them "there was nothing grander than to have his little girls play for him and that together [they] made the most beautiful music this side of heaven." So the girls practiced even when they didn't want to because they adored their father and didn't want to disappoint him. One daughter prayed nightly that God would help her to become what her father seemed to think she already was.[9] Such is the power of persistently encouraging our children.

Consider some of the problem behaviors that plague your family. What steps could you take to encourage your children to change course and choose better?

Loving Children through Good Times and Bad

President George Albert Smith taught that "you can find good in everyone if you will but look for it."[10] The example of our Savior Jesus Christ can teach us much in this area; He spent His ministry reaching out with love, mercy, and compassion to the sinful and the outcast, choosing to believe in the potential of His followers and extending forgiveness for others' mistakes. Unfortunately, saddled with our own mortality, sometimes in our families it can be hard to find the good. Many children go through challenging stages when they make poor choices and are hard to love. During these times it is wise to pray to see your children the way God sees them. Pause and consider what attributes Heavenly Father sees in your children. If your children have received their

8 David Lawrence McKay, *My Father, David O. McKay* (1989), 5.

9 L. Brent Goates, *Harold B. Lee: Prophet and Seer* (1985), 119.

10 *Teachings of Presidents of the Church: George Albert Smith* (2011), 225.

patriarchal blessings, this will give you a few clues. Keep an informal record of insights from other priesthood blessings your child has received. Look for opportunities to encourage your child in developing those attributes.

President Harold B. Lee shared an experience when he chose to encourage someone whose behavior was irksome. On one occasion, he had volunteered to give his daughter a break and take his two young grandsons to a church dance festival. The younger grandson was only five and wasn't too interested in sitting still or watching the program. After President Lee had struggled with the youngster for a few minutes, the grandson doubled up his fist and smacked President Lee on the side of the face. Feeling hurt and a bit humiliated, President Lee paused long enough to remember hearing his daughter say, "You have to love your children when they're the least lovable." So he took his grandson in his arms and told him how much he loved him and wanted him to grow up to be a fine young man. The grandson melted and threw his arms around President Lee. President Lee related, "A successful mother of sons and daughters will tell you that teenagers need to be loved and be loved the most when they are the least lovable."[11]

The more we choose to express love, point out strengths, and compliment character, the more loved and encouraged our children feel.

Finding Ways to Encourage

There are many ways to consciously work to praise and lift our children. Elder Neal A. Maxwell would occasionally write letters to his children specifically praising them and offering light counsel.[12] In our home, we like to write each of our children a letter expressing love, praise, and encouragement every year on Valentine's Day. Sometimes praise and counsel are easier to dole out in a letter, plus the letter becomes something the receiver can cherish as a reminder of your love.

Offering a quick compliment or word of praise can often be short and sweet. Express thanks when a child does something well. Specifically point out a virtue you would like to emphasize, such as selflessness or loyalty. Recognize a child's talent. Give a quick hug or squeeze when you encourage and express love. When children feel loved, they will stay closer to you and home can be a happier place. Everyone rises higher when they are praised and loved.

At times Cameron and I have worked to consistently compliment our children through a little friendly marital challenge. In the evenings or at other times when we are both home together, we will each keep track of how often we sincerely compliment and encourage our children. At the end of

---

11 *Teachings of Presidents of the Church: Harold B. Lee* (2000), 131–32.
12 Bruce C. Hafen, *A Disciple's Life: The Biography of Neal A. Maxwell* (2002), 231.

the evening the parent who was the most complimentary receives a backrub from the other. It's a fun approach that helps us connect with each other while raising the general morale in our home.

President John Taylor taught, "When you get the Spirit of God you feel full of kindness."[13] To the contrary, the natural man often feels that complimenting others somehow lessens his own worth. Pray for the ability to praise and lift others. Look around you for those you know who are good at offering compliments. Study what they say and how they say it. Learning to compliment others has more benefits than just showing love and lifting others. When we sincerely praise those around us, we feel good inside. The Spirit testifies that the choices we are making are good, and we feel full of the Lord's love and more able to love those around us.

Love Equals Time

While expressing love and lifting our children through sincere compliments and encouragement is important, equally as significant is our willingness to give our children our time. Children need to know they can depend on their parents for support; they need parents who are there both physically and emotionally. When President Spencer W. Kimball was a young boy, he would often run into the house from school and call out for his mother. When she responded and asked what he wanted his reply was, "Nothing." He just craved the reassurance that she was there if he needed something.[14] President Thomas S. Monson counseled parents, "I would encourage you to be available to your children. I have heard it said that no man, as death approaches, has ever declared that he wished he had spent more time at the office."[15] Perhaps more than anything else, our time is what signals to our children that they are important. If parents are ready and available to listen to their children, play with them, read to them, and support them through life, children will be more likely to feel loved and secure in their worth.

Most parents know their children need them, but finding and making the necessary time in our daily lives is the tricky part. Consider your schedule and the needs of your children, and map out some good times to regularly connect with your children on an individual basis. Every family and every person is different. When President Harold B. Lee was a school principal at age eighteen, his mother made sure she always had a hot lunch ready for him and was available to talk to him and ask questions about his day's work.

13 *Teachings of Presidents of the Church: John Taylor* (2001), 21.
14 Francis M. Gibbons, *Spencer W. Kimball: Resolute Disciple, Prophet of God* (1995), 14.
15 *Teachings of Thomas S. Monson*, comp. Lynne F. Cannegieter (2011), 211.

President Lee recalled, "This companionship has always continued, and in my manhood I value greatly Mother's wisdom."[16] What a powerful reminder that the relationships we forge in our daily lives when our children are young are but a glimpse of the relationships we will have with them in the future. The time we spend now is a meaningful investment.

When President Russell M. Nelson was a young father, he "maintained a tradition of reading nightly to the younger ones and helping the older ones with their studies so that he was current on their schoolwork while nurturing a cozy relationship."[17]

The when and how will change from time to time as children grow and their needs evolve. Some families work hard to spend a few minutes with each child at bedtime, connecting and discussing the child's day. Some parents let a younger child stay up late once a week to talk or work on a project together. Pray about your current lifestyle and routine, and consider what your children need and what time is available. Sometimes it works best to have set times for individuals every day or every week. Some seasons mandate a more fluid approach; you might keep a notebook, calendar, or list handy and set weekly goals for individual time with each child. Mark off when you achieve a set goal and keep track of how well you manage each week. When you succeed, congratulate yourself. When you don't reach your goal, don't beat yourself up; just keep trying.

One-on-One Outings

One wonderful family tradition that demonstrates love for children is one-on-one outings with a parent and child. Again, there are different ways to do this. Some families have father-child outings; in other families, both parents take turns. One dad I know often takes individual children out for ice cream on the way home from dance or soccer practice. Some mothers check a child out from school once a month or so for a quick lunch date. When Elder Neil L. Andersen of the Quorum of the Twelve Apostles was a young father, he established a tradition of taking each of his children to breakfast each month. His daughter recalled, "He let us pick the place for breakfast and the topics we would talk about. We looked so forward to having his undivided attention."[18]

Outings are a wonderful way for parents to become involved in their children's interests and participate in activities that are enjoyable for them. Let

16 Blaine M. Yorgason, *Humble Servant, Spiritual Giant: The Story of Harold B. Lee* (2001), 60.

17 Spencer J. Condie, *Russell M. Nelson: Father, Surgeon, Apostle* (2003), 92.

18 *Life Lessons from Fathers of Faith,* comp. Gary W. Toyn and Michael K. Winder (2010), 83.

your child choose an activity and set a date on the calendar. Go to a concert, a play, or a game. Play a sport together, go bowling or miniature golfing, or challenge your child to a few games at an arcade. Alternatively you can use the time to help the child work on a skill that interests him. Go to the tennis courts or batting cages; take your child to a fabric store and let her choose fabric for something she would like your help to make. When Elder Neal A. Maxwell's son was interested in baseball and boxing, "Neal practiced baseball with him and then helped teach him to box."[19] One of the sons of Patricia Pinegar recalls telling his mom he wanted to build a robot, and together they cut, colored, and glued a robot costume.[20] Letting your child choose an interesting activity and spending time together sends a clear message of love.

When you are out together, let your children guide the conversation. Talk to them about the things that interest them. Discuss ideas and explore their thoughts and feelings. Ask open-ended questions and soak up the opportunity to show love and get to know your children as individuals. President James E. Faust's grandson recalled that his grandmother read the sports section of the newspaper every day so she would "be able to relate to her grandchildren." Sister Faust acknowledged that "the right to communicate heart-to-heart with each child and grandchild must be earned."[21] I love the example of this wise woman who recognized that she had to learn about the interests of her loved ones to be able to know and love them better.

Giving children individual time, getting to know them through one-on-one conversations, and getting involved with their interests is a key way to earn trust, respect, and love. I love seeing the way my children blossom, smile, and chatter when Cameron or I take them on outings. It is clear that the individual attention shows them how important they are to us. They share more of their hearts with us, and we have a few minutes away from all of life's other pressing needs to focus on listening to and loving each child as an individual. I look forward to these moments when I can be with my children one-on-one.

Personal Time for Parents
Often giving children the time they need requires sacrifices for parents. When President Ezra Taft Benson served as United States Secretary of

19 Bruce C. Hafen, *A Disciple's Life: The Biography of Neal A. Maxwell* (2002), 224–25.
20 Janet Peterson and LaRene Gaunt, *The Children's Friends: Primary Presidents and Their Lives of Service* (1996), 177.
21 James P. Bell, *In the Strength of the Lord: The Life and Teachings of James E. Faust* (1999), 192.

Agriculture, both he and his wife sacrificed to meet the needs of their family. Secretary Benson once chose to forgo one function so he could go to a daddy-daughter party.[22] Another time his wife, Flora, turned down a White House invitation to attend a daughter's choir program.[23] Admittedly these can be tricky waters to navigate. Children have needs, and so do parents. It is easy to let the pendulum swing too far in either direction, with the needs of one party not being met very well. If parents become too wrapped up in their own hobbies and interests, it is easy to let children's needs fall by the wayside. However, if a parent gives all to their family without attending to their own emotional, physical, mental, or spiritual needs, they will not be bringing their full value to the family table. President M. Russell Ballard taught mothers that "water cannot be drawn from an empty well, and if you are not setting aside a little time for what replenishes you, you will have less and less to give to others, even to your children."[24]

When I was in college my minor was marriage, family, and human development. I loved the way those classes prepared me for my future role as a wife and mother. One of the concepts that was emphasized through those studies was the reality of motherhood burnout and the need for mothers to have some outlet for their emotional health—a hobby or interest to inspire them and help them bring fresh eyes to motherhood after brief breaks. Since becoming a mother, it has surprised me how difficult this balance can be. It is easy to feel like there is no time to care for yourself or to feel guilty about taking time for a hobby. Difficult though it may be, it is important to find time to nourish yourself. Coordinate with your spouse or arrange a babysitting swap with a friend or relative, and find something that lifts your spirit. When you do carve out time for yourself, use your time in ways that are rejuvenating instead of time-wasting. Consider how well your chosen outlet feeds your soul, and be careful to choose activities that help you be a better person.

In my motherhood journey I have often drawn on an experience I had when I'd been on my mission for about a year. I had been transferred to an area that wasn't having much success. My companion and I fasted, prayed, and worked, but we didn't see a lot of results for a while, and the battle with discouragement became real. One day my companion and I composed a "happy list"—ten or so simple things that would lighten our mood when

22 Sheri L. Dew, *Ezra Taft Benson: A Biography* (Salt Lake City: Deseret Book, 1987), 299.

23 Derin Head Rodriguez, "Flora Amussen Benson: Handmaiden of the Lord, Helpmeet of a Prophet, Mother in Zion," *Ensign*, March 1987, 19.

24 M. Russell Ballard, "Daughters of God," *Ensign*, May 2008, 110.

nothing seemed to be going well. These were simple items such as listening to a favorite uplifting song or enjoying a bowl of popcorn. On days when things fell apart and we needed to improve our attitudes, we would choose something from our happy list to turn ourselves around.

Many times in my motherhood years I have composed happy lists—simple things that can help me feel better when my day or week has drained my emotional reserves. Many of them have been things I could do while still at home, such as playing the piano or working on a craft project. Some of them have required more planning, such as meeting up with a friend. When I take time for myself, I often rely on this counsel from Elder Dieter F. Uchtdorf:

> The desire to create is one of the deepest yearnings of the human soul. No matter our talents, education, backgrounds, or abilities, we each have an inherent wish to create something that did not exist before. . . . Creation brings deep satisfaction and fulfillment. We develop ourselves and others when we take unorganized matter into our hands and mold it into something of beauty.[25]

The process of creating is a godly desire and activity, and it nourishes our souls. Choosing creative outlets can help me replenish my emotional, mental, and physical reserves. Sometimes I create relaxation and beauty by taking a bath and painting my nails. Other times I create something tangible by knitting, crocheting, or sewing. What creative outlets replenish your soul? Whatever you choose to do when you care for yourself, you will find that taking occasional wholesome breaks will help you feel more loving and give more joyfully to your family.

Listening

Listening is an integral part of spending quality time with children, but it is important enough to merit a bit of individual attention. Elder Robert D. Hales taught, "Research shows that during the most important transitions of life—including those periods when youth are most likely to drift away from the Church—the greatest influence does not come from an interview with the bishop or some other leader but from the regular, warm, friendly, caring interaction with parents."[26] As parents demonstrate that they will listen to

25 Dieter F. Uchtdorf, "Happiness, Your Heritage," *Ensign*, Nov. 2008, 118.
26 Robert D. Hales, "Our Duty to God: The Mission of Parents and Leaders to the Rising Generation," *Ensign*, May 2010, 95.

the feelings, thoughts, and needs of their children, they show love and help children feel their worth.

Wise parents maintain a feeling of respect and open communication with their children in their daily lives. Elder Neal A. Maxwell's son remembered a time when his dad pointed to the two ends of the handle on the oven door and asked, "Tell me how I'm doing as a father. If this on the left-hand side is too strict and the right-hand side is too lenient, where would you say I am?"[27] Such questions teach children that they are important, that their feelings matter, and that you are sincere in trying to help them. When children feel loved and listened to, they will be more likely to open up and share their hearts.

It is important for parents to learn to set aside other priorities to listen to their children at key times. With so many demands vying for parents' attention, this is often difficult. When your child comes home from an activity, try to be available to hear how things went for him. Pause for a minute to establish eye contact. If he is willing to open up, ask appropriate follow-up questions. If your child needs some space, wait for a better time and try again. Demonstrate through your actions that he is important to you. When children are ready to talk, you can have a window into their thoughts, experiences, and feelings.

President Harold B. Lee's daughter recalled going to her parents' bedroom after every date to tell her mother about her evening. She said, "Mother was always interested, so we'd talk and giggle and whisper, and I'm certain that it must have been terribly hard on my father, who would be trying to sleep over the conversation. But he good-naturedly tolerated all of it, for he always encouraged us to confide in Mother. He knew this would build a close relationship, which it most certainly did."[28]

Develop a habit of asking open-ended questions that encourage more than one-word answers. If you ask your children about their day, most will say it was fine and go do something else. If your child is willing, follow up with additional questions to learn what he did that was enjoyable, what happened that was meaningful, and how he felt about things. Many parents ask their children what the best and worst parts of their day were, and these answers can often be followed up with more questions and conversation to understand your child's triumphs and heartaches. I like to ask my children what they did well that day so I can hear about and encourage their talents and successes. Bonnie Parkin taught, "Sometimes it's hard to get more than one-word answers from a teenager. Here's a question that I've found to be extremely helpful in

27 Bruce C. Hafen, *A Disciple's Life: The Biography of Neal A. Maxwell* (2002), 230.
28 L. Brent Goates, *Harold B. Lee: Prophet and Seer* (Salt Lake City: Bookcraft, 1985), 131.

changing that: 'What is the biggest challenge or struggle you have right now?' This question opens the door for youth to share. And when they do, just listen! Don't judge or counsel or anything else."[29]

Sometimes a parent's first impulse after a school day is to ask questions parents tend to worry about. "Did you turn in your homework?" "How was your test?" "Did you talk to your teacher about fixing your grade?" If these are your first questions when you see your child, some children may feel defensive and closed. Although the answers to these questions may be very important, you may be more successful if you create a safe place by letting your child open up about the points of her day that are important to her. This allows your child to feel that you care about her as a person first and not just her academic success.

After asking appropriate questions, learn to listen quietly. Often it is human nature to jump in with our own solutions and values. Communication will flow more freely when we hold back and let children explore their thoughts and emotions. When our children tell us about an experience or person whose values we might question, Cameron will often respond, "What do you think about that?" I have learned that this question allows our children to explore their thoughts without us quickly jumping in to impose our personal values, and we are saved lots of unnecessary preaching if we just listen to our children.

Giving our children the gift of our attention—open ears and a loving heart—is one of the best things we can do. When we share our hearts with our children, communication can remain open and full of love.

Parent-Child Interviews

Many families use weekly, monthly, or occasional interviews as a way to give children individual attention and listen to their thoughts and feelings. Interviews provide a regular opportunity for your children to know they are a top priority and you are ready to hear anything they want to tell you. In some families the father will interview each child; in other families, the parents will do it together or the parents will take turns. Regular interviews enable parents to ask questions, help children set and accomplish goals, and listen intently to their children.

President James E. Faust recommended his children hold personal priesthood interviews with their children, and he held regular interviews with his children and their spouses. His son-in-law relayed, "I was probably a little intimidated by that at first, but what he does, really, is indicate support for us. Everything he says is couched in terms of, 'What can we do to help you?' Those are moments that just draw you to him all the more because you know

29 Bonnie D. Parkin, "Parents Have a Sacred Duty," *Ensign*, June 2006, 96.

that he really has one interest—and that is to help us."[30] What a beautiful example of showing love, support, and availability through listening.

If you would like to have interviews in your family, decide how often you would like to hold them and choose an appropriate time. We like to hold interviews on fast Sunday—it's an easy time to remember and schedule. Some have found it's easier to hold an informal interview when actively doing something with their child—playing a game or going somewhere together. Pray privately before the interview; sometimes, for formal interviews, you can pray with the child during the interview as well. Make these special times to connect with your child. You can start by asking your child what he would like to talk about and just listen. If he is slow to start talking, use a couple of questions to jog the conversation (Appendix 1 has a list of ideas to get you thinking). You might keep a notebook handy during interviews to make an occasional note of something you can do to help a child or an item you need to follow up about. Use interviews as prime times to express love, tell your child you are proud of her, and point out strengths and talents. Ask your child about goals she has or skills she would like to learn, and schedule time to assist with these. Show your child you are on her side and you are there to help her. In some interviews you might learn a lot about a child's life or feelings; other times interviews might be less revealing. But keeping the tradition of regular interviews signals to your children that you want to listen to them, learn about their lives, and support them.

Building a Family Culture of Love

Parents show love for children on an individual basis through listening, talking, spending quality time, and expressing love and encouragement. When children truly feel loved and connected with their parents, home can be a warm, wonderful place. But in addition to showing love on an individual basis, parents can make small choices to foster a spirit of love in their homes between them and their children, between siblings, and in the family as a whole.

Parents help to establish an atmosphere of love through conscious acts of kindness and patience. Kindness and patience are both extremely hard to maintain in families. Children have their own feelings, thoughts, and desires, and helping everyone mesh requires incredible levels of patience. When parents work to be patient with children, love can flow more freely. It can be difficult to consider a child's stage and allow them to develop at their own pace. Every child is individual and matures in unique ways on their own timetable. But when we extend patience to our children, they can feel understood and loved.

---

30 James P. Bell, *In the Strength of the Lord: The Life and Teachings of James E. Faust* (1999), 189.

Greet your children with a smile when they wake up or when they return home. Choose gentle responses. If siblings are bickering or responding sharply to one another or to you, present the change you want to see in your family by demonstrating kindness. Show love and patience rather than nagging or scolding.

Encouraging Sibling Love and Solidarity

In addition to extending patience and allowing children to be individuals, parents can work to create love between siblings. From their children's earliest ages, parents can begin to instill the principle that families are eternal and should be full of love. Homes must provide a safe haven for children, so parents should actively work to prevent siblings from name-calling, put-downs, and fighting. This is a difficult task that requires incredible constancy. When President Ezra Taft Benson's children were young, he and his wife instigated a "no vacant chair" family motto, teaching their children that their family was eternal and each child was cherished and needed.[31] When Mary Ellen Smoot and her husband were raising their children, they "set up family values, and one of those [was], 'As an eternal family we build, support, and edify one another.'"[32] Bonnie Parkin emphasized the phrase "Are you building?" with her sons, expecting them to have a positive attitude, choose wholesome activities, and act as a good influence on each other.[33] When President Gordon B. Hinckley was growing up, his parents frequently reminded the children that "cynics do not contribute; skeptics do not create; doubters do not achieve."[34] Different families adopt different mottos; the important point is that parents teach their children that their family is eternal and must act accordingly.

Many families set up a system of positive reinforcement for good deeds. I know one family who keeps a nickel jar—children's good deeds are rewarded with nickels, and when the jar is full they go out for a treat. Other families use Legos to build a home. Kind words and deeds are recognized with a Lego, and when all the Legos have built a home the family goes out for ice cream. In our family, we maintain a jar of warm fuzzies. Whenever a child pays a sibling a compliment or does something kind or selfless, I encourage that child to contribute a warm fuzzy to the jar. When all the warm fuzzies (about a hundred

---

31 Sheri L. Dew, *Ezra Taft Benson: A Biography* (1987), 130.

32 Janet Peterson and LaRene Gaunt, *Faith, Hope, and Charity: Inspiration from the Lives of General Relief Society Presidents* (2008), 254.

33 Janet Peterson and LaRene Gaunt, *Faith, Hope, and Charity*, 277.

34 Sheri L. Dew, *Go Forward with Faith: The Biography of Gordon B. Hinckley* (1996), 37.

or so) have been put in the jar, our family chooses a special outing as a reward. This is a simple way to recognize children for good deeds and enjoy fun family time. The whole family must work together to earn all the warm fuzzies, and the concept of team effort works behind the scenes to teach children that we are in this life together. If the general morale in our home seems to be low, I can observe a change when I look for any possible opportunity to recognize positive behavior with warm fuzzies.

Parents can also take conscious steps to foster a bond between siblings. From time to time, privately tell a child how important he is in the lives of his siblings. If you have a baby who you notice smiling at her siblings, explain to each older child how much the baby loves them. If you have an older sibling whose example and companionship are important to a younger sibling, point it out on occasion and express how proud you are of your child. Occasional comments from a parent can plant seeds in a child's mind and help shape her view of her siblings. When President Ezra Taft Benson's children were growing up, his wife actively fostered the relationship between their two sons, who were sixteen months apart. Their mother "often told each son in confidence how much his brother loved him. The practice evidently paid dividends, for as unlikely as it may seem, neither brother later remembered ever arguing with the other." One son explained, "Mother's attitude created within me great love for my brother and a desire to work with her to protect him."[35]

If a child is participating in a concert or sporting event, take the whole family along to cheer or encourage. Teach your children that being a cheerleader is part of being a sibling.

Teaching Children to Love Parents

Additionally, parents can work to foster love between children and their parents. President David O. McKay taught that the most important thing a father can do for his children is love their mother.[36] When parents are united, children are blessed. All marriages include some level of compromise, but contentious issues should not be discussed in front of children. Do the best you can to provide your children with a united front. If an issue becomes sensitive, agree to revisit the topic later in privacy. Speak highly of your spouse as much as possible, and don't emphasize or complain about flaws. Do the best you can to give your children an opportunity to love both of their parents regardless of shortcomings. Demonstrating loyalty by not complaining or

---

35 Sheri L. Dew, *Ezra Taft Benson: A Biography* (1987), 129.
36 Cited by Elaine S. Dalton, "Love Her Mother," *Ensign*, Nov. 2011, 77.

focusing on mistakes also teaches your spouse and children that they can trust you. Everyone has flaws, and no one likes having theirs highlighted.

Allowing children to love both of their parents can become difficult in cases of divorce or other deep challenges. In many of these cases, one parent is helpless to protect children from the choices of the other parent. It becomes difficult not to vilify a current or former spouse whose choices hurt other family members. One dear single-mother friend shared that she tries to remember the importance of a father's role in the eyes of her children. Despite his choices, she recognizes that when she demeans her former spouse in front of her children, she hurts her children and forces them to choose sides. Often the choices of an errant parent are confusing, embarrassing, or painful enough to children, and they should not be asked to also deal with the hurt feelings of their other parent. By refusing to vent her frustrations in front of her children, my friend provides her children a more secure foundation and the opportunity to forgive and love their father despite hurtful choices.

Mothers can teach their children to love their father through her example. When President Russell M. Nelson was a young father, his wife would prepare their children for his homecoming each day by saying, "'Okay, girls, let's pick up all your toys so the house will be clean when Daddy comes home. And when he walks through the door, let's all give him some hugs and kisses.'"[37] In our home, we have trained our children to give Cameron a royal send-off in the mornings. Everyone gives him a hug and a kiss and stands to wave goodbye in the garage. In the summer, the kids often run down the street and wave from the corner. Cameron feels like a king when his little party is standing on the corner waving him off in the morning. Such family traditions foster love, happiness, and unity.

Loving Children's Friends

Finally, parents can establish homes filled with love through a culture of accepting and welcoming their children's friends. As children grow, friends become increasingly important. By inviting your children's friends over, you get to know these friends and you demonstrate love and acceptance of your children. Parents might not always like their children's friends, but loving your children and being involved in their lives is still an important choice.

President Howard W. Hunter's wife, Claire, encouraged her sons to bring their friends home and made sure food was available for them.[38] President Ezra

---

37 Spencer J. Condie, *Russell M. Nelson: Father, Surgeon, Apostle* (2003), 60.
38 Eleanor Knowles, *Howard W. Hunter* (1994), 114–15.

Taft Benson's wife, Flora, "preferred that the children bring their friends home to play" and worked to make home "more enticing than anywhere else."[39] President Harold B. Lee's daughter recalled that their "home was always open at any time of the day or night to our friends. We came to appreciate parents who made that possible." She concluded, "Now that I am a parent I probably realize fully for the first time that this type of involvement with friends frequently in our home could have been an inconvenience. I'm certain that many times we must have disturbed our parents when we'd sing round the piano and giggle and laugh and talk, but they never complained."[40]

Sometimes having children's friends over isn't convenient—groups can become loud or messy. But opening your home, graciously greeting your children's peers, and warmly getting to know them provide significant long-term benefits. You get to know your children's friends, provide a safe environment for their socializing, and demonstrate love for your children. These social groups allow you to understand and influence your children's world a little better. Everyone's home situation is different. Many have small living spaces, tight grocery budgets, or other limitations. Consider your circumstances, and work within your constraints to welcome your children's friends and get to know them better.

Love is the foundation of any happy family. As a parent, you know how much you love your children. Demonstrating your love through quality individual time, listening, encouraging, and building a family culture of love and acceptance can fill your children with a deep sense of worth and peace.

---

39 Sheri L. Dew, *Ezra Taft Benson: A Biography* (1987), 134.
40 L. Brent Goates, *Harold B. Lee: Prophet and Seer* (1985), 131.

Application

1. If you aren't currently holding interviews in your family, consider how they might work best for you. Determine a workable schedule, and put the interviews on your calendar.
2. When you interview a child, take notes and follow up on appropriate items.
3. How might parent-child outings work best in your family? Plan these each month.
4. Set a goal to be a better listener. Ask your children how they feel about events they share. (Refer to Appendix 1 for examples of open-ended questions.)
5. Ask your children occasionally if they feel you listen to them. Work to make appropriate changes.
6. Set a goal to work on patience and kindness with your children.
7. Privately tell each of your children how important they are to their siblings. Teach them to cheer for each other both at home and at public events.
8. Choose a family motto that unifies your family and teaches children the eternal nature of your family.
9. Work to make your home hospitable for your children's friends.
10. Express love to your children every day.
11. Make a conscious effort to look and smile at your children more often.
12. Consider whether implementing a family system for positive reinforcement (such as warm fuzzies or a nickel jar) would be encouraging for your children.

CHAPTER 8
Compassion

Kindness is the essence of a celestial life. —*Joseph B. Wirthlin*[1]

I THINK IT IS SIGNIFICANT that the family proclamation includes both love and compassion as attributes of successful families. Some might think of love and compassion as being two sides of the same coin. Most parents love their children, and many parents work to demonstrate that love. Compassion, on the other hand, is sadly absent in much of the world. It can be extremely challenging for parents to consistently demonstrate compassion toward their children. When the needs of children are added on top of financial, marital, medical, or other stresses, compassion is often the first thing to slide. We can't provide our children with a perfect world, solve all their problems, or give them everything they want. Sometimes our first response is to explain the facts with heavy doses of reality and only minor traces of sympathy. When compassion falls apart in families, often so will mutual respect. Soon love, forgiveness, and other wholesome values also disintegrate.

We see the opposite example in the life of our Savior, Jesus Christ. When their brother Lazarus died, Mary and Martha wept in sorrow and disillusionment. The Savior went to raise Lazarus, but He wept as He did (see John 11:35). Christ had compassion for Mary and Martha and their sorrow even though He knew that in a moment he would turn their sorrow to joy. He didn't tell them not to cry. He didn't tell them He was going to make everything better. He wept with them. What a profound lesson for parents who seek to have compassion and to comfort their children.

Christ demonstrated similar compassion among the Nephites. After tenderly teaching the Nephites following His Resurrection, the Savior told them the time had come for Him to return to the Father. But when the Savior

1 Joseph B. Wirthlin, "The Virtue of Kindness," *Ensign*, May 2005, 26.

saw the tears in the eyes of the multitude and sensed their tremendous desire for Him to stay, He said, "Behold, my bowels are filled with compassion towards you" (3 Nephi 17:6). What followed is one of the sweetest scenes of Christ's ministry as he healed the afflicted and personally ministered to each individual child. Truly we worship a Savior who is touched by our feelings and experiences.

As parents, it can be hard to follow the Savior's example of pure compassion for our children's desires and feelings. How do we develop greater compassion in our own hearts? How do we teach our children to have compassion? Let's explore some doctrine and examples.

Compassion, Tenderness, and Kindness

If we want to raise children who are tender, compassionate, and kind, we must treat our children and others with love and kindness. President Spencer W. Kimball taught, "There is a constant need to develop and to maintain tenderness. The world's ways harden us. The tenderness of our women is directly linked to the tenderness of our children."[2] What a powerful statement! The first and most important way to maintain and teach compassion in our homes is to work to build it in ourselves.

Daily family life presents countless opportunities for parents to choose to see situations through the eyes of their children and extend kindness and compassion. President Spencer W. Kimball's son recalled their family occasionally returning home late at night, and he would feign sleep so he wouldn't have to go out and milk their cow. Sometimes his father kindly let him sleep and milked the cow himself.[3] When President Brigham Young was a child, he often went to bed hungry, so when he became a parent, he ensured he always had a well-stocked pantry for hungry children.[4] President Joseph F. Smith walked the halls at night for hours with a sick child.[5] President Gordon B. Hinckley's mother stayed up all night with him when his ears ached.[6] President Harold B. Lee's parents sometimes pulled their children out

---

2 Spencer W. Kimball, "Privileges and Responsibilities of Sisters," *Ensign*, Nov. 1978, 104.

3 Edward L. Kimball and Andrew E. Kimball, Jr., *Spencer W. Kimball: Twelfth President of the Church of Jesus Christ of Latter-day Saints* (1977), 149.

4 Lynda Cory Robison, *Boys Who Became Prophets* (1998), 10.

5 *Teachings of the Presidents of the Church: Joseph F. Smith* (1998), 295.

6 Sheri L. Dew, *Go Forward with Faith: The Biography of Gordon B. Hinckley* (1996), 24.

of bed at night to give them oven-fresh bread with honey and milk.[7] After his family left Nauvoo, President John Taylor risked his life to go back and rescue his child's favorite toy rocking horse.[8] All of these examples—some minor and some requiring considerable sacrifice—teach children to treat others with compassion and tenderness.

What does the daily routine look like in your home? Where are the glitches where your children might appreciate a touch of kindness or empathy? Recognizing small but important moments and choosing to extend love and compassion teaches your children to be softer. As you demonstrate compassion for your children, they will know how to treat others (including their siblings) with compassion.

Cameron has often spoken of his experiences as a teenager with a mother who actively looked for ways to demonstrate compassion in their home. When he showered before school in the morning, his mother would occasionally throw a towel in the dryer and set it out for him. After his shower he would have a nice, warm towel ready and waiting. What a sweet example of showing love and compassion in a simple occurrence.

President Harold B. Lee's daughter recalled that when she and her sister were young, their father carried them to bed so they wouldn't have to walk on the cold floor of the sleeping porch. There he tucked them in snugly and expressed words of love. She said, "I have often thought about that expression of father love to us and ever will be grateful that love, security, and tenderness were planted deep in our hearts."[9] More than words or actions demonstrated to others, showing compassion in daily life for our children allows Christ's doctrine of compassion to sink deep into their souls.

Compassion and Family Harmony

Demonstrating compassion for our children in life's everyday ups and downs teaches a significant doctrine. But parents who live lives of compassion at home do more than teach doctrine—they also affect family harmony in powerful ways.

President Harold B. Lee's daughter Helen remembered an occasion in her teen years when she and her sister were supposed to return home together from a Church function at a specific time. When the time came to leave, her sister Maurine refused to go and encouraged Helen to go home alone. When

7 Blaine M. Yorgason, *Humble Servant, Spiritual Giant: The Story of Harold B. Lee* (2001), 39.

8 Amie Jane Leavitt, "The Love of a Father," *Friend*, March 2010, 21–22.

9 L. Brent Goates, *Harold B. Lee: Prophet and Seer* (1985), 117.

Helen arrived home alone, her parents immediately began to confer about how to handle Maurine's disobedience. Their father was ready to march back and make sure his daughter understood the importance of exact obedience. Their mother suggested they first wait to see if their daughter returned. When Maurine didn't quickly return, President Lee insisted that he had to go and help her understand that she had to do what she was asked to do. Their mother gently encouraged him to not make a scene or embarrass the daughter in front of her friends. She suggested he come up with another reason for returning to the church. "Don't go in an angry way and insist that she come home," she counseled.

Helen wasn't there to see what happened, but when her father and sister returned, Maurine was in a wonderful mood and didn't seem to feel embarrassed or upset. Helen said, "Through the wise handling of tense situations in this manner, discipline in our home never degenerated into the abrasive confrontations that are common today in too many homes."[10] As her parents counseled together and Sister Lee advocated for compassion in considering Maurine's feelings despite her disobedience, harmony and love at home remained intact. Boundaries for children's behavior must be enforced, but choosing to maintain rules with love and compassion can make all the difference in family harmony.

In addition to treating errant children with compassion, we can choose to extend empathy when our children make mistakes or choices we don't immediately agree with. When Elder David B. Haight's son was young, he was involved in a car accident that was his fault. When he called to tell his father about the wreck, his father demonstrated compassion. Responding calmly and without condemnation, he simply told his son to "take [the car] down and get it fixed."[11] As tempting as it is at times to remind a child that you knew his choice would bring problems, this doesn't convince him you are on his team. When our children make mistakes, do we think of how they are feeling and try to hold our tongues?

When Belle Smith Spafford, former Relief Society general president, was invited to the junior prom, her widowed mother had only four dollars to spare—enough to buy satin for a new dress or a textbook Belle needed. Belle's mother let her choose, and of course Belle chose the dress. Her mother went to work making a pink satin dress and bought matching pink slippers. Later she quietly told Belle, "You know that textbook is in the school library." Many years later, as she recalled the experience, Belle stated that her mother's choice

10 L. Brent Goates, *Harold B. Lee: Prophet and Seer* (1985), 132–33.
11 Lucile C. Tate, *David B. Haight: The Life Story of a Disciple* (1987), 153.

to support Belle's wishes to get the dress was "a very wise decision, because for a girl in high school it was important."[12] Rather than pressuring her daughter to focus on her studies, Belle's mother considered the event through the eyes of her child and let Belle choose. She then helped Belle make the most of her choice.

President David O. McKay's son shared how his father's compassion affected his behavior. Father and son were out in a horse-drawn carriage and were caught in a thunderstorm. The son recalled, "I thought the end of the world had come, and started to cry. Father held me on his lap in his arms all night until we were rescued in the morning. It's hard to disobey a man who loves you and puts his arms around you."[13] I believe there is a sermon in that statement. If we want our children to obey us, we must show love and compassion for them. Demonstrating compassion teaches doctrine, but it also builds family harmony. When children feel their parents' love, demonstrated through acts of compassion, they may more naturally respond with love, respect, and obedience.

Beautiful things can happen in a parent-child relationship when the child feels like her parents understand her and have compassion for her feelings and experiences. Considering your child's situation, feelings, and concerns and demonstrating compassion shows your child she can trust you with her heart. President Joseph F. Smith addressed this topic when he taught parents, "Convince your children that you love them, that your soul goes out to them for their good, that you are their truest friend." He promised parents that if you can do this, children "will place confidence in you and will love you and seek to do your bidding and to carry out your wishes with your love."[14] Think about the implications of this promise. President Smith encouraged parents to help children feel that their parents are their truest friends. How often do you treat your children as your friends? Do you laugh with them, work to spend time with them, and listen to them with the intent to understand? It is easy for parents to fall into habits of nagging and commanding rather than listening and empathizing. While it is critical for parents to teach and train their children by setting appropriate expectations, boundaries, and consequences, it is also important for parents to be their children's friends. Most of the time it is easy to treat our friends with compassion as we try to understand situations through their eyes. Do we extend the same grace to our family members?

12 Janet Peterson and LaRene Gaunt, *Faith, Hope, and Charity: Inspiration from the Lives of General Relief Society Presidents* (2008), 160–61.

13 *Teachings of the Presidents of the Church: David O. McKay* (2003), 153.

14 *Teachings of the Presidents of the Church: Joseph F. Smith* (1998), 299.

As much as I try in everyday life to be kind to my children, from time to time it is helpful for me to specifically focus on kindness and compassion for a week or two. When I do, I always find room to improve. Compassion in families is difficult to maintain amidst daily demands. But when I work extra hard to show compassion for my children, I notice that I am a happier mother.

One afternoon my son was complaining to me about his schoolwork and how much was required of him. In his eyes, his burdens were too much to bear. My first response was to explain in rather unsympathetic terms that he still needed to do his work. I worried he was being too sloppy and careless in his assignments. However, as our conversation progressed, I quickly saw that his response to my lacking compassion was to close off emotionally, and I realized I wasn't being the kind of parent I wanted to be. Pausing to remember my own concerns with heavy homework loads when I was his age, I took a few minutes to empathize about what he was facing. When I did, I felt more love for my son and more hope as well. My son warmed up and shared more of his feelings. I realized I had been approaching the encounter from a fear standpoint instead of with love, compassion, and encouragement. Of course, this didn't instantly solve my son's school concerns. But it did help both of us feel better. Choosing compassion with your children allows them to feel closer to you and safer trusting you with their feelings and concerns. The more you choose compassion, the better you will feel about your child and yourself. As you demonstrate compassion, the Lord will fill you with love and the presence of His Spirit.

When we show compassion, we think about how the other person is feeling. We accept their feelings as valid and important. We reach out with open hearts and loving hands. Accepting others' feelings and reaching out to lift those around us is work. Sometimes as parents we feel overwhelmed by all the needs and feelings our children exhibit. Sometimes we can't make it all better for a child. But you can watch for specific triggers that lessen compassion as you monitor tenderness and compassion in yourself.

Avoiding Labels

Assigning a negative label to a child, either in public or in private, is a sign of diminished compassion. If a parent tells a child she is lazy or is a pain, a liar, a bully, or even shy, the child will internalize a negative self-concept. These sorts of labels can lead children to feel flawed, discouraged, or unlovable. Name-calling or assigning negative labels to children will often prompt them to behave more in a way that reflects the negative label. Elder Lynn G.

Robbins taught that "we must be careful not to say things that would cause [our children] to believe that what they *did* wrong is who they *are*. . . . Our children are God's children. That is their true identity and potential. His very plan is to help His children overcome mistakes and misdeeds and to progress to become as He *is*. Disappointing behavior, therefore, should be considered as something temporary, not permanent—an act, not an identity."[15]

Sometimes as parents we think we are clever. We might not label a child in that child's presence, but in private conversations with a spouse or friend we might refer to a child as irresponsible, rebellious, stubborn, or obnoxious. The child may not hear these labels, but sometimes this doesn't solve the problem. Children are often more perceptive than we realize. When parents silently feel resentful or critical, children can still pick up on it. Additionally, when we mentally assign labels to a child, we often hurt ourselves. If we consistently categorize our children in these ways, we may unconsciously shift ourselves into a victim mindset; our children become the bad guys. If this happens, compassion fades and we may convince ourselves our children are beyond our help. We may stop feeling a need to work so hard to love and guide them. We sometimes may even convince ourselves our children are undeserving of our assistance and compassion.

Often a child who is misbehaving is feeling discouraged. When children feel good inside, they make good choices. As parents we can choose to see our children, spouses, and ourselves as works in progress. All children have strengths, weaknesses, and quirks, just as we do. All children go through challenging phases. The trick for parents is to work to maintain compassion, consider the world through their children's eyes, think of what might be causing the behavior, and pray about how to help them. Instead of labeling your children, pray about what actions might help your children feel better inside. What silent needs are they expressing? What actions might help them feel loved and encouraged?

Overcoming Selfishness

Sometimes the root of lacking compassion is selfishness. When children's needs become difficult to meet, parents may tell themselves children are demanding too much, and they turn off their heart. When this happens, parents quickly convince themselves they are right and their children are wrong. With so many voices in the world telling people to take care of themselves, it isn't

---

15 Lynn G. Robbins, "What Manner of Men and Women Ought Ye to Be?" *Ensign*, May 2011, 104, emphases in original.

a hard jump to make. In these times it is wise to pause and ask if the action you are considering is what the Savior would do. Jesus daily demonstrated kindness and compassion, and these are important attributes for parents to develop. When a child's needs are overwhelming, instead of turning off your heart, turn to Christ. Plead in the moment for His strength so you can extend a bit more love, patience, or kindness. Let His grace lift you.

Kindness, gentleness, and compassion demand incredible strength. Demonstrating compassion in small acts or bigger manifestations sometimes isn't easy for parents. But choosing a lifestyle of love and kindness teaches children the importance of following the Savior's gentle example of love and service.

The prophets placed respect, love, and compassion in that order in the family proclamation. When parents demonstrate respect for their children through their words and actions, love can flow. It is possible to love someone you don't respect, but love flows more easily when respect is mutual. Respect and love are each demonstrated through acts of compassion.

Compassion Challenge

At one point in time, I was concerned about the levels of compassion being demonstrated between siblings in our home. After discussing the matter in family council, we agreed to a family compassion challenge. For one week we would all try to stop what we were doing when someone was sad or hurt so we could listen, hug, comfort, or support the person. This exercise increased compassion among our children, but I also noticed a change in myself. Sometimes as parents it is hard to pause what we are doing to demonstrate compassion. Often we are busy cooking, cleaning, working, or addressing other tasks. But determining to drop what you are doing to hold, hug, listen to, or comfort someone can help you become a softer, kinder parent. President Thomas S. Monson's timeless words are an appropriate reminder for all parents: "Never let a problem to be solved become more important than a person to be loved."[16]

Setting the Example

Demonstrating compassion for our children in their daily lives is an essential first step in establishing homes filled with compassion. The next step is for parents to demonstrate compassion for others. Children are keen observers. If parents consistently serve and lift those around them, their

---

16 Thomas S. Monson, "Finding Joy in the Journey," *Ensign*, Nov. 2008, 86.

children may notice and eventually imitate their parents' lives of compassion. Parents should be alert to the needs of others if they want compassion to take root in the hearts of their children.

President Thomas S. Monson "attributed his desire to lift those in need to the example of his mother." [17] During the Great Depression, his family was frequently visited by those who needed a meal. President Monson recalled, "I saw my mother minister to those men, totally unafraid, no fear in her at all. . . . That same spirit carried forward with me. I have had great satisfaction in pursuing that same spirit of helping others."[18]

President Monson's wife, Frances, had a similarly generous mother. Frances recalled being taken to a department store once as a girl to get a new dress and coat. Because it was during the Great Depression and many had fallen on hard times, her mother also bought a dress for one of Frances's friends whose parents couldn't afford one.[19]

When Elder Neal A. Maxwell and his wife, Colleen, were raising their children, Colleen worked to teach her children a "service perspective." She "visited people in need and invited to dinner a steady stream of members of the student ward, widows and widowers, or others she felt needed a little friendship." At times her children admittedly would have preferred fewer visitors. Over time, however, they began to appreciate the wisdom behind their mother's habits of service.[20]

When Sister Marjorie Pay Hinckley was growing up, it was not uncommon for her to come home to find a note explaining that someone else was sleeping in her bed. Her father was kind and compassionate and no matter "how depleted their pantry was, [he] couldn't turn anyone away hungry."[21]

Such lifestyles of generosity and awareness of others' needs sink deeply into the hearts of children. Service and sacrifice can be hard to accomplish, especially when families are busy trying to take care of their own needs. Usually the years when parents have children at home are filled with packed schedules and frazzled, weary parents. Yet the quiet acts of kindness parents perform don't go without their rewards. Some of those rewards may come in future generations as children teach grandchildren to love, serve, and show compassion.

---

17 Adam C. Olson, "Maintaining the Course," *Ensign*, April 2008, 13.
18 Olson, "Maintaining the Course," 13–14.
19 Heidi S. Swinton, *To the Rescue: The Biography of Thomas S. Monson* (2010), 92.
20 Bruce C. Hafen, *A Disciple's Life: The Biography of Neal A. Maxwell* (2002), 229.
21 Sheri L. Dew, *Go Forward with Faith: The Biography of Gordon B. Hinckley* (1996), 112.

If service and compassion are not an inherent part of your current lifestyle, consider some minor adjustments you can make. Pray for opportunities to serve those around you. Ask the Lord to give you eyes to see needs. Set a goal to perform meaningful service each week. Celebrate your successes, and share appropriate stories with your family at dinner. As you consistently serve others, your burdens will feel lighter and you will feel happier. Service is the essence of a Christ-centered life.

Demonstrating Compassion through Callings

A prime vehicle for parents to teach service and compassion is through Church callings. These service opportunities often require sacrifice as parents strive to care for their families and serve well in their callings at the same time. Many blessings come quietly in these years as service to others in callings becomes an understood way of life.

Elder L. Tom Perry grew up while his dad was serving as a bishop of their ward. He specifically remembered his father selflessly ministering to a widower. Before the man passed away, he left a letter of gratitude to Tom's father. Young Tom watched his father read the letter after the man's passing with tears rolling down his cheeks and "understood a little better what it means to serve God and His children."[22]

When President Gordon B. Hinckley's wife served as ward Relief Society president, she was often busy serving a sister in their ward with cancer. Her daughter remembered that as a time when her mother was often not home after school. But she also noticed that her mother would come home "so full of pure love." She later said, "I love Church work. Is it any wonder with a mother like that?"[23]

When Ardeth Greene Kapp was growing up, her father served as bishop and her mother worked hard to facilitate that service. She recalled, "Mom always did behind-the-scenes things, and we were always cheering Dad on. It was not until later we came to realize that Mom was always in the wings, playing a major role."[24]

President Hinckley's daughter was taught to love Church service through the pure example of her mother. Elder L. Tom Perry learned to serve from

22 Lee Tom Perry, *L. Tom Perry: An Uncommon Life, Years of Preparation* (2013), 68.

23 *Glimpses into the Life and Heart of Marjorie Pay Hinckley,* ed. Virginia H. Pearce (1999), 30–31.

24 Anita Thompson, *Stand As a Witness: The Biography of Ardeth Greene Kapp* (2005), 42.

watching his father. Ardeth Kapp learned about service and sustaining others through her parents' examples.

As evident from these Church leaders, children learn what to expect and how to behave from their parents' examples. Your actions now may prepare your children for future service in Church callings. Such was the case with Zina D. H. Young, third general president of the Relief Society.

When Zina was little, her family lived in Kirtland. Frequently her mother "without direction or prompting from any one" would take little Zina "in her buggy and hunt out the distressed and needy." If someone needed something Zina and her mother couldn't supply, they would "travel among the people, in and out of the Church" to find it. "Thus early was 'Little Zina' inducted into the spirit and mission of the Relief Society, although it then had no existence."[25]

It may be hard to tell right now what your lifestyle of service can mean to your children. You may teach them to notice and serve those around them. You may be unconsciously preparing them to serve faithfully in a Church calling, help spouses with their callings, or minister to someone in need. As you serve those around you, the doctrine of compassionate ministry to those around them may sink into your children's souls. Compassion is a principle that can seep through generations to the benefit of many in and outside your family tree.

Teaching Children to Serve

When parents live lives of service, demonstrating compassion for their children and those around them, the stage is set for a final step: involving your children in service opportunities.

Some opportunities for service are minor but meaningful. When President Thomas S. Monson was a child, he remembered going to a store at Christmastime and seeing a man ringing a bell and asking for donations. Young Tommy's mother deposited a coin in the container and then turned to her son and asked if he would like to donate as well. He gave all he had—two nickels.[26]

At one point, Elder Neal A. Maxwell's wife, Colleen, volunteered their son to help a neighboring widow by taking her garbage can to the curb each

---

25 Orson F. Whitney, *History of Utah*, as cited in Janet Peterson and LaRene Gaunt, *Faith, Hope, and Charity: Inspiration from the Lives of General Relief Society Presidents* (2008), 63.

26 Heidi S. Swinton, *To the Rescue: The Biography of Thomas S. Monson* (Salt Lake City: Deseret Book, 2010), 47.

week. Although he protested a bit at this opportunity, his mother explained the value, and he followed through.[27]

Both of these examples are minor acts of service a parent can encourage children to perform. Minor acts of service can begin to inscribe a love of service in children. Teach your children to be aware of those around them. Help your children feel comfortable looking for needs and offering to serve.

Teach your children the doctrine of service. Service is the essence of discipleship, a key way for us to keep our baptismal and temple covenants. Christ constantly served others when He was on earth. Serving others shows that we are serious about following our Savior. Plan a family home evening lesson to teach the doctrine of Christlike service. Share stories of how Christ served others. Encourage family members to follow Christ's example and look and pray for opportunities to help those around them.

A simple place for children to begin serving is in the home. Help your children notice their siblings' needs. Encourage and praise their efforts to help at home. Teach them you are proud of their efforts to serve and be selfless.

Help your children serve alongside you so they can enjoy time with you and feel the joy of service at the same time. When Elder L. Tom Perry's father served as a bishop, he often involved young Tom in ministering to needs. Often when Tom returned home from school, he would find an assignment his father had left him, fill his little red wagon with necessary items, and make deliveries. At times his father would accompany him, and these became precious memories.[28]

Brother Tad R. Callister remembered his father often taking him to visit the elderly, pick up food for them or give them money. Being involved on these excursions filled Tad with a desire to serve like his dad did.[29]

As a young father, President George Albert Smith worked to teach his children service and compassion one Christmas. After the gifts were opened, he asked his daughters if they would like to give some of their toys to some children who hadn't had a Christmas. At first the girls volunteered to give away their old toys. With some gentle coaching, they eventually chose a couple of new ones, and together father and daughters delivered the gifts. President Smith knew his daughter had caught the joy of service when she said, "Now let's go and get the rest of the toys for them."[30]

27 Bruce C. Hafen, *A Disciple's Life: The Biography of Neal A. Maxwell* (Salt Lake City: Deseret Book, 2002), 229.

28 Lee Tom Perry, *L. Tom Perry: An Uncommon Life, Years of Preparation* (2013), 67.

29 Tad R. Callister, "Parents: The Prime Gospel Teachers of Their Children," *Ensign*, Nov. 2014, 33.

30 *Teachings of the Presidents of the Church: George Albert Smith* (2011), xix.

Teaching children to serve and show compassion requires a bit of thought and work but is wonderfully satisfying for everyone involved. In the process your children can feel the joy of lifting others as Christ would do. Families, wards, and communities are often full of service opportunities. Keep an eye open for expectant or new mothers or people with health challenges or other grief who might benefit from a warm meal; involve your children in preparing and delivering the food. Heart attack (tape paper hearts onto someone's door) or write notes to those you see who could use uplifting. When possible, involve your children in visiting widows or shut-ins. Teach your children that life presents a variety of challenges to all of us and that these are opportunities for us to extend love and kindness.

Serving in the Community

Finding service projects outside your immediate circle of friends and acquaintances requires a bit of sleuth work but is certainly possible. An easy first step is to sign up for notifications from justserve.org, a website sponsored by the Church that can notify you of current service opportunities in your area. You can download the app to your phone or sign up for weekly emails. Or you can browse for projects in your area that are suited to your specific needs. Check with local hospitals, shelters, refugee centers, and food pantries to see if there are services your family can provide. Many hospitals appreciate blankets or other donations. Food pantries sometimes need help sorting or delivering food to shut-ins. Refugee families might appreciate simple donations or mentors to help them adjust to a new country and culture. Local homeless shelters often need volunteers to serve meals to their patrons. When our children were young, we discovered the Ronald McDonald House, which allows us to bring our family in to prepare and serve a meal to families staying there who are enduring medical challenges. Our family deals with an unusual variety of medical concerns, so it is easy for us to have compassion for these people. Through the years, our children have enjoyed talking to many Ronald McDonald House patrons. We have been able to follow up this service by encouraging our children to pray for some of these families whose stories have touched their hearts.

Another wonderful method for inculcating service into your family culture is to help your family set a service goal each year. Our family holds a family retreat every January. Fashioned after the model of a corporate retreat, we spend a night at a hotel to make it feel official. We hold a few meetings (with lots of snacks) and set family goals, discuss family values, set family standards, and share training items. In between meetings we swim, play, watch movies, and go out for meals. It has been our habit to set a service goal each year at our family retreat. When our children were small, we often felt good with two or three solid service projects a year. One year our son suggested we aim for a hundred acts of service for people outside our family. Admittedly, we felt a bit dubious, but we decided to accept his challenge. Each week in family council we discussed acts of service family members had performed that week: taking people meals, going to the temple, indexing, visiting those who were sick or grieving, helping people move, shoveling others' driveways in the winter, or raking leaves in the fall. We were surprised and pleased at how quickly our list of service projects grew—and we all felt good about what we had accomplished.

Jesus Christ lived a life of constant service—endlessly teaching, healing, and extending love and compassion. Elder Joseph B. Wirthlin of the Quorum of the Twelve Apostles taught, "Kindness is the essence of greatness and the fundamental characteristic of the noblest men and women I have known. . . . Jesus, our Savior, was the epitome of kindness and compassion."[31] If we are serious about our discipleship, we will be serious about serving those around us as Christ would do. As we serve our family members and others, we can teach our children to do the same. Teaching our children to have compassion and serve others prepares them for lives of joy as they minister and serve as Christ would do.

31 Joseph B. Wirthlin, "The Virtue of Kindness," *Ensign*, May 2005, 26.

Application
1. Look for opportunities to demonstrate compassion for your children in everyday life. Service and sacrifice speak their own sermons.
2. Notice and identify triggers when you feel yourself closing your heart to your child. How can you soften to show more love?
3. Avoid labeling or categorizing children publicly or privately.
4. Issue a family compassion challenge. Whenever someone is hurting, encourage family members to drop what they are doing to hug or comfort the one in need.
5. Set a service goal for yourself and pray to see those around you who are in need. Be aware of those around you who could use love, friendship, or a helping hand. Your children will notice your kindness.
6. How might your current Church calling teach your children about compassion? Involve your children in related service activities when appropriate.
7. Plan a special family home evening about service. Teach your children the doctrine of Christlike service, and encourage them to pray for opportunities to serve others.
8. Involve your children in service projects. Invite them to serve or volunteer to help others.
9. Look around your community for available service opportunities at food kitchens, hospitals, refugee centers, homeless shelters, or other charities. Sign up on justserve.org to receive notifications of local opportunities.
10. Help your family set a service goal. Be ambitious! Enjoy tracking your success.

CHAPTER 9
Work

Teaching children the joy of honest labor is one of the greatest of all gifts you can bestow upon them.[1]*—L. Tom Perry*

MY HUSBAND, CAMERON, HAD A wise grandfather who served as bishop of a singles ward at Brigham Young University. Whenever a couple would approach Grandpa to announce their engagement, he would give them one piece of initial counsel: go work together for a day. He kept lists of elderly people or others who might appreciate young people who could help with some hard labor. Some of these young couples went to work for a day and reported back on their experiences with glowing terms, feeling confident and even more in love. Some couples spent a day working together, realized they didn't work very well together, and decided that perhaps their marriage wouldn't be a good idea. When Cameron started to think about marrying me, he arranged for us to help a friend drywall his basement and build a new shed. We spent hours together working one Saturday, and at the end of the day we felt even more optimistic about our relationship. Many times through the years we have reflected on the wisdom of Grandpa's counsel. Families present boundless opportunities for hard work—sometimes physical and sometimes emotional, mental, or spiritual. Having a marriage in which the two partners work harmoniously on projects is helpful. Teaching children to then follow that example and work hard is the next worthy challenge.

Have you ever wondered why work is spiritually important? When the Lord sent Adam and Eve forth from the Garden of Eden, He told them He would curse the ground for their sake (see Moses 4:23). This curse of the ground meant Adam and Eve had to work, something that perhaps they had not done as much in the Garden of Eden. Why did God make work requisite for His children here on earth?

1 L. Tom Perry, "The Joy of Honest Labor," *Ensign*, Nov. 1986, 62.

First, work is godly. Work is what God does. God described His work in Moses 1:39: "For behold, this is my work and my glory—to bring to pass the immortality and eternal life of man." Caring for His children and leading them home is God's work. Our Father in Heaven does not sit idly by in the heavens—He works, and He works for our salvation. Learning to work hard and work well is just one way we learn to be more like Him.

Additionally, if we wish to return to our eternal home, we all have quite a bit of work to perform. Gaining and maintaining a testimony is work. Serving others as Christ would serve is work. Discipleship is work. Truly, we believe in a gospel of work. Our Father in Heaven gave us a world where work is a requirement so we can learn the joy of labor. Learning to work blesses us physically and spiritually.

Lessons from Work

Admittedly, although work is hard, teaching children to work is harder still. Many parents feel it's easier to do jobs themselves. Unfortunately, choosing this route deprives children of countless essential life lessons. President Thomas S. Monson has encouraged, "Mothers, share household duties. It is often easier to do everything yourself than to persuade your children to help, but it is so essential for them to learn the importance of doing their share."[2] Work is often the best way to instill virtues of gratitude, contentment, diligence, thrift, and financial responsibility. Work is a powerful teacher, and wise parents recognize that it is a wonderful gift to give their children.

Let's take a quick look at some of the lessons afforded by hard work.

Gratitude

One of the first lessons that hard work can teach is gratitude. Sometimes love propels us to want to shower our children with material comforts. But when we do so we often deprive them of the joy of working for something. If you want something badly enough to earn it, you prize it because of the sacrifice it cost you.

The Lord placed us on an earth that would grant us the opportunity to learn to work hard and value what we earn. In previous generations, this lesson was driven home through work like farming. Eating meant working to plant, water, nourish, and care for a garden over a period of months before any food would be available. But working to eat taught people to appreciate what they grew.

2 *Teachings of Thomas S. Monson,* comp. Lynne F. Cannegieter (2011), 210.

Parenthood operates in a similar way. Long hard months of pregnancy with all of its aches, pains, and discomforts or years of infertility, heartache, and adoption processes precede the joy of bringing a child into your family. These months of sacrifice bond parents to their children and fill their hearts with love and a willingness to continue to serve. Would parents be ready to accept the extreme sacrifices, heartaches, and difficulties of parenthood if they weren't required to sacrifice so much in the beginning? We love and value the things we work and sacrifice for. Allowing children to experience the blessings of yearning, working, and sacrificing is a powerful gift parents can give.

Diligence, Responsibility, and Exactness

Providing your children with copious work opportunities is also an essential way to teach values such as diligence, responsibility, and exactness— qualities all good parents want their children to develop.

Elder Neal A. Maxwell remembered his father as being "loving but exacting." In contrast, Elder Maxwell described himself as a youth as "a stranger to excellence." One day he decided to earn his father's praise and approval by installing some fence posts with exactness. "I worked hard all that day and then scanned the lane expectantly down which my father would walk home. When he arrived, I watched anxiously as he carefully inspected the fence posts, even checking them with a level bar before pronouncing them to be fully satisfactory. Then came his praise."[3] Young Neal learned to rise to his father's standard of excellence.

Elder L. Tom Perry's mother also taught her children lessons of diligence and exactness. When her children cleaned a room, her instructions were always the same: "Be certain you clean thoroughly in the corners and along the mopboards. If you are going to miss anything, let it be in the center of the room." She knew things left in the center of the room wouldn't be neglected, so she taught her children to clean well the areas that otherwise might be overlooked. Elder Perry said, "Over the years, my mother's counsel has had enormous application to me in many different ways. . . . It is in the hidden corners of our lives where there are things that only we know about that we must be particularly thorough to ensure that we are clean."[4]

In the long run, it is better if parents insist on teaching their children lessons of exactness, diligence, and responsibility. Parents can teach and train with love and patience. While the process may be exhausting, it is better than

---

3 Neal A. Maxwell, "'Put Your Shoulder to the Wheel,'" *Ensign*, May 1998, 37.
4 L. Tom Perry, "Discipleship," *Ensign*, Nov. 2000, 60.

hoping your children will somehow absorb such lessons from future teachers, employers, or spouses.

Despite your best efforts, children will still have to learn some lessons of exactness through natural consequences. When President Gordon B. Hinckley and his brother were growing up, it was their responsibility to "empty the water as it melted from the icebox in the cellar." Being young boys, they often forgot and "spent more time cleaning up the water that had overflowed the small pan than would have been required to take it out in the first place."[5] But life on their family's farm included plenty of opportunities to learn diligence and responsibility through hard work. The family orchard had a wide variety of fruit trees that produced generously. In January and February, the boys and their father spent Saturdays pruning. In the summer and fall, fruit "had to be picked, graded, packed, and sold." Through all this work year after year, "an important lesson . . . embedded itself in Gordon's subconscious: the quality of fruit picked in September is determined by the way the trees are shaped and trimmed in February."[6] Most families today cannot provide orchards to teach their children lessons of work and responsibility. But parents can still furnish children with consistent opportunities to learn work, exactness, diligence, and responsibility.

Thrift and Contentment

Parents can also consciously teach their children lessons of thrift and contentment. Whatever your income and financial status, you can set the example by living joyfully within your means. Don't covet all the shiny, fancy goods that are advertised. Learn to care for what you have and to feel content. Sometimes as parents it is easy to fool ourselves into believing we are giving our children more when we want newer and bigger. In reality, showing our children how to live with love, joy, and contentment is a greater gift.

Like responsibility and diligence, thrift was taught naturally in previous generations. President Harold B. Lee grew up on a farm situated on a dirt road. "Money was dreadfully scarce in those days. . . . But the Lee children did not know they were poor." To the contrary, President Lee described his childhood family as having "everything money could not buy."[7]

Ardeth Greene Kapp grew up in Canada in a frugal home. One year the family's turkeys were all killed by a hailstorm, making money especially tight.

---

5 Sheri L. Dew, *Go Forward with Faith: The Biography of Gordon B. Hinckley* (1996), 26.

6 Sheri L. Dew, *Go Forward with Faith*, 27.

7 *Teachings of Presidents of the Church: Harold B. Lee* (2000), xii.

When Christmas drew near, Ardeth longed for a chenille bedspread. "I didn't actually expect anything under the Christmas tree, and I understood why, but I couldn't help mentioning it anyway," Ardeth recalled. Her father's response was gentle and wise: "My dear, if we could get one for you, my concern is that if you get used to luxuries like this you might expect them and it would be hard for you when things get tough." Although Ardeth got the bedspread for Christmas, she admitted her father's counsel was an important lesson.[8]

President Spencer W. Kimball drew an insightful connection between work and covetousness in the lives of our children. "Too much leisure for children leaves them in a state of boredom, and it is natural for them to want more and more of the expensive things for their recreation. We must bring dignity to labor in sharing the responsibilities of the home and the yard."[9] Providing children with plentiful work teaches them to value what they have and curbs covetousness. Parents can teach children through word and deed that money doesn't buy happiness and less is often better.

Financial Awareness

Finally, ensuring children work opportunities both in and outside the home can teach them financial awareness. President M. Russell Ballard encouraged families to "have a simple family economy where children have specific chores or household duties and receive praise or other rewards commensurate to how well they do. Teach them the importance of avoiding debt and of earning, saving, and wisely spending money. Help them learn responsibility for their own temporal and spiritual self-reliance."[10] Elder Marvin J. Ashton of the Quorum of the Twelve Apostles agreed that "children should earn their money needs through service and appropriate chores." Speaking against an unconditional allowance, he went on, "I think it is unfortunate for a child to grow up in a home where the seed is planted in the child's mind that there is a family money tree that automatically drops 'green stuff' once a week or once a month."[11]

Elder Lynn G. Robbins shared that, in their family, chores and responsibilities were split up into things that were expected of everyone (such as cleaning their rooms) that weren't paid; things that contributed to the family's workload (such as cleaning up after a meal or vacuuming) that were

8 Anita Thompson, *Stand As a Witness: The Biography of Ardeth Greene Kapp* (2005), 17.
9 Spencer W. Kimball, "The Stone Cut without Hands," *Ensign*, May 1976, 5.
10 M. Russell Ballard, "What Matters Most Is What Lasts Longest," *Ensign*, Nov. 2005, 43.
11 Marvin J. Ashton, "One for the Money," *Ensign*, Sept. 2007, 37.

paid; and optional chores that were well paid, such as weeding the garden or cleaning the windows. Their children were responsible for purchasing their own clothing and other personal items. "Enough opportunities were made available to them so they could earn all they needed if they would just work."[12]

When children are young, parents can decide on a system to help their children earn money for their needs. Some families pay their children for grades. Others pay them according to their performance in assigned household tasks. Some make lists of available jobs for children to complete and earn money accordingly. Decide how and when you would like to help your children begin to understand financial skills. What tasks are you comfortable paying them for? What would you like them to be responsible for purchasing? Allowing your children to work, earn money, and spend it wisely is a wonderful way to introduce them to the value of a hard-earned dollar and teaches them to care for their possessions.

We like to introduce our children to our family financial system sometime around age eight. They earn money according to how well they perform their normal household tasks or additional chores they volunteer for, and they are responsible for buying their own clothes and other necessities. In the beginning our children typically feel the opportunity to earn and spend their own money sounds terribly grown-up and exciting, and we couch it in terms of trust and responsibility. They soon discover that wise financial management grants them freedom to buy things when they need and want them. We have observed that allowing children to begin earning their own money and to be responsible for their purchases is a tremendous vehicle for teaching them to save, budget, and spend wisely. When children begin to earn their own money and manage their finances, they can begin to understand the importance of saving for future needs and caring for current investments.[13]

Expecting Children to Work
Parents should expect their children to work around the house with regular responsibilities. Elder D. Todd Christofferson of the Quorum of the Twelve Apostles has said that "all honest work is the work of God."[14] (Doesn't that sound like a great quote for your refrigerator?) Furthermore, President Spencer

---

12 Lynn G. Robbins, *Love Is a Choice: Making Your Marriage and Family Stronger* (2015), 188–89.
13 If you are looking for a complete system to teach your children financial responsibility, I recommend reading *The Entitlement Trap* by Richard and Linda Eyre.
14 D. Todd Christofferson, "Reflections on a Consecrated Life," *Ensign*, Nov. 2010, 17.

W. Kimball taught, "We want you parents to create work for your children."[15] I ponder that statement sometimes. It is not enough to just include children in the normal work that must be done around a home—we must create work for them to do! From time to time it is wise to consider your family system. Where are the glitches that need to be addressed? What other jobs could be shared to make the road a bit smoother?

At one point in time, I was trying to figure out how to share the workload of breakfast preparation with our family. Our menu options had fallen into a deep rut of items people were tired of eating, and I was out of ideas. After a bit of brainstorming on how to involve everyone in this task, we formed the Sullivan family breakfast club. Once every few weeks, in family council, we choose which foods to prepare, and I buy the appropriate groceries. Then we choose a weekend time slot to prepare breakfast mixes and foods together. We all work together to prepare waffles or breakfast burritos to freeze, bake homemade granola, and make pancake or muffin mixes. It's fun to work together, and we are rewarded with a bunch of nice breakfast options. Working together as a family feels good. And as a bonus, our children gain extra kitchen experience.

Are there facets of family life work that are becoming too heavy? How can you share the workload with the rest of your family?

Of course, it is important to recognize that your children will not always cheer when you give them work to do. They might not thank you for a couple of decades, if they do at all, and they will probably drag their feet and complain. Persevere. As much as they may balk, "children need to know that they are part of the family engine and not the baggage."[16] In the long run, work gives children skills and confidence. In the short run, work teaches your children they are essential members of your family unit. Teach them that not only do you love them and enjoy spending time with them but that you need their talents and efforts to make your family stronger.

Designating Work Times

Many families designate specific time slots for work to be done. Traditionally many families have set aside Saturday mornings for housecleaning and yard work. When Elder L. Tom Perry was growing up, "Saturday morning was a time set apart for house cleaning, and everyone participated." After cleaning the bedrooms, everyone pitched in to clean up the rest of the house as well. Their mother would follow up to make sure tasks were completed exactly.[17]

15 *Teachings of the Presidents of the Church: Spencer W. Kimball* (2006), 120.

16 Margaret D. Nadauld, *A Mother's Influence* (2004), 44.

17 Lee Tom Perry, *L. Tom Perry: An Uncommon Life, Years of Preparation* (Salt Lake City: Deseret Book, 2013), 59.

At our house, our children know they are expected to clean their rooms every Saturday and help with other specific tasks that are assigned as needed. Over time, as this has become our routine, we have had less resistance and more cooperation. When work time is consistent, children may complain a little less. (Any minor whining and complaining that persists may just remind you your children really are children and not robots.)

In previous generations, many families woke up early to manage farm chores and other important tasks. When President Gordon B. Hinckley was growing up, his father generally woke up by five and expected his children to follow suit. "There were always plenty of chores for the boys, and each day they could plan on receiving a list of jobs to be done by noon."[18]

President Joseph Fielding Smith taught his children that "people die in bed. And so does ambition." Every morning he and his wife woke up the children by six, and everyone "did their part to keep the house clean and organized." One son shared, "Somehow it seemed immoral to Dad for us to lie in bed after six o'clock. Of course, I only tried it once. Father saw to that."[19]

Some families still observe an early-morning habit of cleaning. If this will work in your home, choose certain tasks children are expected to have completed before breakfast, school, or other activities.

In our home, it works well to expect our children to have tasks done by mealtime (usually dinner) or bedtime. A half hour before dinner I ask them to tidy up and make sure the house is ready for dinner. A clean house at dinnertime makes the whole evening feel better. Other privileges, such as playing with friends or enjoying screen time, are similarly tied to expectations of completed chores and school work.

Ponder your family's needs and situation, and consider what should be cleaned and when—Saturday mornings, weekday mornings, or weekday evenings. Choosing a system gives children consistent responsibilities and establishes a routine to help everyone thrive.

Training Your Troops!

An inherent part of expecting your children to work is providing adequate training so they understand how to properly complete each task. This is a process that takes much time and patience.

Elder L. Tom Perry shared a lesson he learned about teaching his children to work. When his son was young, he began to teach him how to weed. Elder

---

18 Sheri L. Dew, *Go Forward with Faith: The Biography of Gordon B. Hinckley* (1996), 26.

19 *Teachings of the Presidents of the Church: Joseph Fielding Smith* (2013), 288.

Perry assumed his son would be good at weeding since he was low to the ground, but he soon discovered his son had a hard time recognizing weeds and leaving vegetables alone. He experienced similar frustration teaching his son to milk a cow. His son would soon be sitting in a white puddle with an empty milk bucket. Elder Perry shared, "I was frustrated. I expected him to help me, but he only seemed to create more work." (Isn't that a sentiment any parent can relate with?)

Finally Elder Perry recalled his own childhood experiences and the work his father exacted of him, which hadn't seemed to make sense at the time. "I began to understand. Work is something more than the final end result. It is a *discipline*. We must learn to do, and do well, before we can expect to receive tangible rewards for our labors."[20] As parents, our task is to teach our children to do and do well, and this is usually a long, thankless process. However, as we expect our children to work and teach them how to perform assigned tasks, we give them the gift of confidence.

Parents must remember that, as overwhelming as the present years may seem to them, they are perhaps raising a future missionary, a future spouse, and a future parent. What are the tasks your child will need to master to excel in these situations? Both boys and girls should be taught to cook, sew, clean, iron, do laundry, and complete basic home, car, and yard maintenance. As our children grow up and leave home, they will be prepared to provide for themselves and exercise righteous stewardship over the blessings the Lord grants them. Training and expecting children to work prepares them for the future lives they may build.

Usually teaching a child to do a job well is a process that takes several exposures. Start by deciding what you want your children to know how to do and when you will teach this. What are the tasks your children should be introduced to at their age? Are your children old enough to be taught how to do their own laundry? Should your children learn how to clean their own bathroom? Is it time for your children to be taught the finer points of vacuuming a room well? Consider when you can start teaching them these skills. For instance, often I will choose a few tasks I want to train my children to do in the summer when their schedules are a bit more relaxed. Additionally, throughout the school year, we will help them set goals to master certain tasks, and then together we will focus on training them in those tasks. If you are married, counsel with your spouse in your family executive council about what tasks each child might be ready to learn and who would do best at teaching them.

Once you have decided the what and when, start by showing your children how to complete a task well. Sometimes it is worth demonstrating a task two

20 L. Tom Perry, "The Joy of Honest Labor," *Ensign*, Nov. 1986, 63–64.

or three times and talking to your children about the process as you go. Explain what you do and why it's important. Answer questions and quiz your children for understanding. Ask them to repeat back what needs to happen.

After these initial demonstrations, monitor your children completing the task as many more times as necessary. Watch to make sure they do things properly. After your children have mastered a skill, it is still wise to check to make sure they do the task well and don't slip into bad habits. Be exact, but be merciful and consider your children's ages and abilities. Your children may not do everything the way you would. But your efforts help them learn discipline and develop skills. This process is hard work for both of you but well worth the investment.[21]

Limited Family Councils

We like to use limited family councils to encourage our children to develop the skills they want when they are interested. President M. Russell Ballard explained that limited family councils are a time for both parents to sit down with one child to counsel, discuss current concerns and future decisions, and set goals.[22] If you are a single parent, you can accomplish the same objectives when you sit down with a child individually. In our home, these are generally short, sweet, informal sessions that happen on Sunday after breakfast or before bed (depending on what time we have church). We discuss what goals they would like to focus on for the coming week and how they would like to accomplish them. Each child has a small whiteboard to record their goals on; sometimes they draw boxes on their boards to check off during the week when they have accomplished their objectives. We encourage our children to keep these goals simple—one or two goals a week is generally sufficient. Of course, not all of their goals relate to new skills they want to master. And our children don't always perfectly follow through on their initial ideals. But we enjoy the process of teaching them to ponder and set goals and consistently work toward them.

Sometimes our children know what they want to work on. If they want ideas, we will probe with a question or two: Is there a new skill you would like to work on? Is there something you would like to learn about? This is also an excellent time to help our children set and achieve goals for various Church programs. Our children's goals have ranged from exercise objectives to reading about a new topic to learning to prepare a new recipe to making a

---

21 For a comprehensive list and system for training your children on appropriate tasks, I recommend *The Parenting Breakthrough* by Merrilee Boyack.

22 M. Russell Ballard, "Family Councils," *Ensign*, May 2016, 64–65.

new friend or inviting someone over to working to be more consistent with personal prayers or scripture study.

Cameron and I have learned to treasure these short, one-on-one council sessions in which we can focus on each child and how they feel about life. We congratulate them on any successes from the previous week and express how proud we are of their progress and then probe for how we can help when goals aren't achieved. We love the way these simple goal-setting sessions teach them to be constantly growing and improving.

Working Together

As you are training each child in specific tasks and in everyday jobs that must be addressed around your home, try to maximize the moment. Working together builds relationships and grants opportunities to connect one-on-one. If you are cleaning the kitchen or working on a task with just one child, savor the time to talk to him. Listen to his thoughts and get to know him better. Consider the experience from your child's point of view.

President James E. Faust said that "work became a joy when I first worked alongside my father, grandfather, uncles, and brothers. I am sure that I was often more of an aggravation than a help, but the memories are sweet and the lessons learned are valuable."[23]

When President Gordon B. Hinckley's children were growing up, his oldest son looked forward to Saturdays as a time when he and his father "repaired, remodeled, planted, and planned."[24] These days spent working together also served as quality time to build their relationship.

Bonnie Parkin shared that she loved to garden with her sons one-on-one in the early-morning hours. "We talked a lot about life and its challenges. It was a very safe place for my sons."[25]

What will your children remember about working by your side? Will they remember you talked to them, listened to them, and shared your heart with them? Are your children forming tender memories while you sort laundry together?

Similarly, working together on a project as a family provides valuable time to bond and build relationships within a family group. Help your children

---

23 James P. Bell, *In the Strength of the Lord: The Life and Teachings of James E. Faust* (1999), 467.

24 Sheri L. Dew, *Go Forward with Faith: The Biography of Gordon B. Hinckley* (1996), 161.

25 Janet Peterson and LaRene Gaunt, *Faith, Hope, and Charity: Inspiration from the Lives of General Relief Society Presidents* (2008), 277.

savor the sense of accomplishment as together you achieve cleanliness and order. When you are finished, point out how much you have accomplished and how good it feels to do a job well. Teach your children to notice the joy of finishing a task.

On one occasion, my mission president shared a fact about marriage that pertained to mission companionships. "You grow to love your spouse because of everything you go through together," he said. Likewise, he taught, missionaries love their mission companions because of all the experiences they share. As spouses (or mission companions) work together for a united purpose, love grows. The same principle applies to families. When families learn to work together, a beautiful synergy occurs. Something powerful happens when family members learn to roll up their sleeves and go to work together. Families build relationships, memories, and love one shovelful of snow, one garbage bagful of leaves, and one load of dishes at a time. At the time, your children may drag their feet and beg to be done, but in years to come, they may recall with fondness the times the family worked together toward a common goal.

Such was the experience of Barbara Winder, former Relief Society general president. She shared that as a child she did not appreciate their family's garden and the work it required. Later she reflected, "I didn't know then, as we snapped the peas and shelled the beans preparatory for canning, that more than a winter's storehouse of food was being preserved. We were laying foundations for family relationships that would be much greater than our year's supply. In fact, we are still being richly fed from those seeds planted many years ago."[26]

If your children balk and complain when you work together as a family, press forward. Know you are achieving something far more lasting than a good day's work!

Keeping Things Light

Finally, while you are exerting such efforts to teach your children the value of work, remember to keep things as light and pleasant as you can. Children will not always respond happily to work assignments. Say please and choose gentle persuasion over power struggles.

President Gordon B. Hinckley's oldest son, Richard, remembered having one particular chore as a child that became his nemesis. His mother would ask him to please take out the wet garbage (food scraps to be deposited in the compost), and he would slide down the wall and play dead or pretend to be

---

26 Janet Peterson and LaRene Gaunt, *Faith, Hope, and Charity: Inspiration from the Lives of General Relief Society Presidents* (2008), 205–206.

in pain. He recalled that his mother, "ever patient, would just laugh and say, 'Well, when it begins to spill out of the sink and fill the kitchen, I guess we'll just have to eat in the living room!' No coercion, no raised voice, certainly no corporal punishment; just a shrug of her shoulders and a suppressed laugh." Eventually, of course, he would complete his task.[27]

I love that mother's example of lightheartedness and gentle expectation. In a scenario when many would feel tempted to resort to threats, punishment, or power struggles, her easy manner kept everything okay. And the task still got done.

Consider some ways to make family work time a bit more enjoyable. If the whole family is cleaning the kitchen, turn on some happy music and see how many songs it takes to get everything done. At times our family has had dishwasher races and timed ourselves to see how long it took us to unload a dishwasher. We kept track of our times for a little while, and our speed definitely improved. If your children are young, use some creativity to motivate them. Pretend that in five or ten minutes a terrible witch or beautiful princess will be coming to your house and you have to get ready. Or ask your children to surprise you and show you how well they can clean a room without your help. Then heap on the praise when the job is done well.

When Bonnie Parkin and her husband were raising their four boys, they would play Beat the Clock to see how quickly they could finish a task.[28] Another version of a time challenge is to set a timer for ten minutes and see how much everyone can get done. Our house can make a dramatic recovery if everyone works consistently for ten minutes.

Elder Neal A. Maxwell's son remembered raking leaves with his dad and then leaping into them and laughing together.[29] Similar spontaneous enjoyment can be had from water fights after washing the car or indoor snowball (sock-ball) wars after folding the laundry.

When President Russell M. Nelson was a young father, "he would preside at Saturday night baths with a 'four-in-a-tub-shampoo-train.'" He would pour water and a bit of shampoo on each head and then instruct his girls to massage each other's heads. After a minute he would say, "About face," and the girls would turn around and scrub the head of the sister who had previously been scrubbing them. "The shampoo train was an elementary lesson on the Golden

---

27 *Life Lessons from Mothers of Faith,* comp. Gary W. Toyn (2012), 14.
28 Janet Peterson and LaRene Gaunt, *Faith, Hope, and Charity: Inspiration from the Lives of General Relief Society Presidents* (2008), 276.
29 Bruce C. Hafen, *A Disciple's Life: The Biography of Neal A. Maxwell* (2002), 224.

Rule."[30] It also made a simple task easy, fun, and a delightful source of happy childhood memories.

If you are cleaning together on a Saturday, plan for a fun family game or outing together after all the work is done. Some Saturdays are naturally busy for families—sporting events, music lessons, or errands can dominate the day. Do the best you can with the time you have available. Play a game, go on a picnic or hike, have a cookout, or go on an outing. Such scheduling naturally teaches children that work comes before play.

Margaret D. Nadauld shared that when her sons were growing up, her husband would wake them up early every Saturday morning. One son recalled, "If there were in fact no pressing chores, we would simply move dirt. It was Saturday morning, and we were working: that's what mattered to him." After a while they would stop, and he would take the boys water skiing. "After a couple hours of dragging [them] around the lake in an old boat . . . he'd stop in the middle of the water for lunch. Then, as [they] were all sitting there, his captive audience with bologna sandwiches in one hand and sodas in the other, [he] would teach [them]." Although his sons didn't realize at the time all their father was accomplishing, they learned to embrace the values he taught through word and action.[31] Chief among those values were the satisfaction that comes from good hard work and the love that grows from playing together afterward.

Teaching children to work is work. Putting forth the effort to appropriately train and involve your children will pay rich dividends as your children gain skills and confidence and your family builds memories working and succeeding together.

---

30 Spencer J. Condie, *Russell M. Nelson: Father, Surgeon, Apostle* (2003), 69.
31 Margaret D. Nadauld, *A Mother's Influence* (2004), 63–64.

Application

1. Decide on a family financial system. How would you like to help your children earn money?
2. Designate specific time slots for work to be done. Decide what should be done when, and develop a consistent routine with individual tasks assigned to each family member.
3. Once or twice a year review your current family system. What areas should be revisited for better efficiency? What jobs should be delegated differently? What tasks require more thorough training?
4. Follow President Spencer W. Kimball's advice to create work for your children.
5. Periodically help your children set goals of tasks they would like to learn and spend adequate time training them. Utilize summer breaks and other free times to help your children develop extra skills.
6. Hold regular limited family councils to help your children set and achieve goals.
7. Look for opportunities to visit with your children one-on-one as you work together. These are priceless moments to ask questions and listen with your heart.
8. How can you make work opportunities more enjoyable? Consider games or creativity you could introduce to keep the environment light.
9. Schedule outings or family playtime after family work time.

CHAPTER 10
Wholesome Recreational Activities

Family time is sacred and should be protected and respected.
—Boyd K. Packer[1]

I THINK IT IS ONLY fitting that after extolling the virtues of work in the previous chapter, we spend a lighthearted chapter focused on playing together as a family. The prophets knew what they were doing when they ordered these nine principles, didn't they? Work is vital, but so is play. As essential as it is for parents to teach their children to work responsibly and diligently, it is perhaps equally critical for families to play together. Just as beautiful memories are built as we work together, wonderful memories are built as we play together. Parents must work to schedule and preserve time for family members to be together, enjoy each other's company, and build happy memories. Let's consider some ways to accomplish these objectives in our families.

Avoiding Overscheduling

For years prophets have counseled parents to not overschedule their families. In today's world there is tremendous pressure for parents to enroll their children in a staggering number of lessons and activities. Some parents might feel guilty for not involving their children in enough opportunities or pushing them to explore more talents. However, too many commitments in a family can lead to overtaxed, unhappy family members. Freeing up our family calendars can give more time for family members to bond and enjoy each other and can enable parents to feel happier and more relaxed. Additionally, the Spirit can reside in our homes more when family members feel less pressure and more joy. Fewer commitments can mean more time to be still, to enjoy each other, and to feel the sweet presence of the Spirit in our lives and homes.

---

1 Boyd K. Packer, "And a Little Child Shall Lead Them," *Ensign*, May 2012, 9.

In generations past, children had more freedom to follow their natural creativity and explore their environments. When President Gordon B. Hinckley and his wife were raising their family, they owned a large piece of land with gardens and orchards, and Sister Hinckley worked hard to keep summer days open for her children to explore and savor. One day when everyone was working, they couldn't find their oldest son, and Sister Hinckley recalled that "all afternoon [she] practiced a speech [she] would give him when he showed up." Predictably, he showed up at mealtime, and she inquired where he had been. He responded that he had been down in the ravine doing nothing.

She didn't give him her speech, and many years later she was grateful. When college finals were crushing in and young-adult pressures felt intense, he came home one day and said, "I had a wonderful childhood, didn't I?"

His mother responded, "Well, I hope so. You did your share of complaining about all the work that had to be done."

He went on to reminisce about long summer days lying on his back listening to singing birds or watching ants hard at work. When life's pressures felt overwhelming, he was sustained by memories of simple, carefree childhood summers. Sister Hinckley summarized by saying, "Things are different now. Children hear so many voices from so many directions. There are so few empty summer days. There are pressures to excel. It has become a challenge to let children be children. It has never been so important that children have a home that is a place of refuge."[2]

How do we as parents create homes of refuge where children can be children? It can be easy to get carried away signing up children for one more class, lesson, or group. Consider your schedule carefully and prayerfully. With each new activity, a little more stress is generally added to the family structure. While we may think our children need one more lesson or camp, sometimes what they really need is more time to connect with their family members and enjoy a sanctuary where they feel loved and secure.

Every few months it is helpful to consider your family's schedule. Analyze each activity with its pros and cons. Talk to your children and pray together about which groups or lessons are most beneficial to them. Don't be afraid to cut out extras. Your child will probably grow up just fine without an extra few months of trombone lessons or another year of dance class. With family commitments, less is often more.

---

2 *Glimpses into the Life and Heart of Marjorie Pay Hinckley,* ed. Virginia H. Pearce (1999), 53–55.

Managing Screen Time

One prominent detractor of quality family time is screen time. It is easy for parents and youth to get sucked into distractions on phones or screens. In *For the Strength of Youth* we are cautioned with this timely advice:

> Take care that your use of media does not dull your sensitivity to the Spirit or interfere with your personal relationships with others. Spending long periods of time using the Internet or a mobile device, playing video games, or watching television or other media can keep you from valuable interactions with other people. Be careful that your use of social media does not replace spending time with your family and friends.[3]

It is important for parents to discipline themselves and then seek to discipline their children in this regard. Parents can choose a variety of boundaries for themselves to set a good example for their family and make sure their children receive the focus they deserve. For instance, you can limit your checking of email, social media, or other online sites to once or twice a day, hopefully in a time slot when family members need less from you. If items arise throughout the day that you might want to look up online, jot a note to yourself. By the end of the day you may have a list of things you need to do online. You can take care of all of them in a consolidated timeframe rather than allowing yourself to be distracted from your family during the day. This allows you to focus on your family and tasks of greater importance. During dinner and other family times, set aside phones and enjoy the opportunity to look at family members and listen to them. Limit how much time you spend on computer, phone, and videogames in a day. Appropriately limiting your own media usage sets a good example for your children.

Elder Gary E. Stevenson has cautioned, "The use of social media, mobile apps, and games can be inordinately time-consuming and can reduce face-to-face interaction. This loss of personal conversation can affect marriages, take the place of valuable spiritual practices, and stifle the development of social skills, especially among youth." He went on to encourage parents to "teach and demonstrate the righteous use of technology to the rising generation and warn against the associated hazards and destructive use of it."[4]

Realize that when your children spend time on screens watching TV, playing games, surfing Internet videos, or checking social media, they have less

3 *For the Strength of Youth* (2011), 12–13.
4 Gary E. Stevenson, "Spiritual Eclipse," *Ensign*, Nov. 2017, 46–47.

time to connect with family members and others in ways that can help them feel hopeful, loved, and worthwhile. Screen time can never provide our youth with the love and validation they crave. Phones and other screens have the potential for good as we stay in touch with loved ones or learn new worthwhile things through programs found online. An occasional show provides parents of young children a longed-for reprieve and time to get a few things done. Family movie nights can accomplish important goals of family togetherness. But parents have a responsibility to set healthy boundaries for themselves and to guide their families in their media use.

There are a variety of ways to help youth manage screen time wisely. Many parents put a limit on how much screen time a child can have in a day and require school work and household jobs to be finished first. Some families require their youth to sign a contract outlining family rules before they receive their own phones. Parents may require their youth to check their phones in for the night in their parents' room and communicate all passwords with parents. Others lock their children's phones down to just phone calls and text messaging. Some offer phones as a basic tool and ask their children not to give their phone number out to others.

Media and screen time standards are an important discussion item for family council so that parents and children can truly listen to each other. Teach your children that when you help them manage their screen time, you are trying to give them a gift of love and the opportunity to build stronger relationships with those around them. On occasion, ask your children how they feel you manage your personal screen time. Do they feel like you focus on them at the right times and set appropriate boundaries for your own phone or other media use?

Some parents might consider finding a moment when a child is in a good mood and receptive to counsel to have a basic discussion about how screen time makes them feel. Question your children about how they feel after family game night or a fun outing with friends. Also ask how they feel after spending time surfing the Internet or playing computer games. Generally, too much time on a screen is numbing to our spirits. Healthy time spent with others is the opposite—it provides feelings of connection, love, and hope.

Cell phones and other devices are modern conveniences with great potential for good. Choosing to manage our screen time and teaching our children to do the same can help us stay grounded in gospel principles and focused on what matters most. Sister Bonnie L. Oscarson, former Young Women general president, has taught,

We live in a culture where more and more we are focused on the small, little screen in our hands than we are on the people around us. We have substituted texting and tweeting for actually looking someone in the eye and smiling or, even rarer, having a face-to-face conversation. We are often more concerned with how many followers and likes we have than with putting an arm around a friend and showing love, concern, and tangible interest. As amazing as modern technology can be for spreading the message of the gospel of Jesus Christ and helping us stay connected to family and friends, if we are not vigilant in how we use our personal devices, we too can begin to turn inward and forget that the essence of living the gospel is service.[5]

We must teach our children to put their screens away and notice the needs of others. Helping our children monitor their screen usage better prepares them for joy in future roles as missionaries, employees, spouses, and parents.

Give your child the gift of time to explore, create, build, and imagine. Silence your media and enjoy each other. Read books together. Play in the park. Go on a hike. Let them think and play. I like Marjorie Hinckley's advice:

> You may not be able to take them on exotic vacations. It doesn't matter. When the day dawns bright and sunny, take an excursion to the canyon or park. When it's cloudy and wet, read a book together or make something good to eat. Give them time to explore and learn about the feel of grass and the wiggliness of worms. . . . As you create a home, don't get distracted with a lot of things that have no meaning for either you or your family.[6]

In a world where children are flooded with so many voices, quality time to be home with family, soaking in a gospel culture and enjoying talking and playing with parents and siblings, is often more beneficial in the long run than additional extracurricular activities or screen time.

Scheduling Play

Freeing your calendar of unnecessary commitments and distractions is the first step to creating quality time. The next step is to actively schedule time

---

5 Bonnie L. Oscarson, "The Needs before Us," *Ensign,* Nov. 2017, 25.

6 *Glimpses into the Life and Heart of Marjorie Pay Hinckley,* ed. Virginia H. Pearce (1999), 75–76.

for your family to be together playing, building relationships, and forming memories. Every week in family council, assess your calendar for the week. Vigilantly consider times when you can schedule family playtime.

Every family will gravitate toward different forms of play. Choose what works well for you. The important point is that you do it. Some families choose quiet activities. When President Howard W. Hunter was growing up, his father would pull out the family's encyclopedia and say, "Where shall we travel today?" With atlas and encyclopedia in hand, they would tour the world from their living room, and young Howard became well acquainted with countries, states, and capitals.[7]

President David O. McKay worked to balance his busy schedule by playing baseball with his boys and reading to his younger children. "He loved to sit in the chair with the children on his lap and read to them *The Lady of the Lake, Ivanhoe,* or *The Bluebird.* The children were especially delighted when he spoke in Scottish dialect." In this way the children were well versed in classic literature, and "quotations and stories flowed through the family."[8]

As a young father, Elder Neal A. Maxwell developed a habit of entertaining his children with stories he made up about Tweedle-Dee, Tweedle-Dum, and "Friends of the Forest." He continued the tradition with his grandchildren and savored the opportunity to just lie down on the carpet, put his arms around them, and tell them stories.[9]

When President Thomas S. Monson was a mission president, he kept a relentlessly busy schedule. But every night he would invite his son into his office and challenge him to three games of checkers. His son recalled, "He'd let me win one, then he'd beat me at one, and then we'd play give-away checkers and either one of us could win that. But he did that almost every night and . . . that meant a lot to me as a kid."[10]

Some families choose more active forms of play. President John Taylor's son remembered that his father "had a strong desire to keep his children under the family influence and provided play grounds for us. Even when he was past seventy years of age he would join us in our games. He provided a large sand pile for the little ones and if I have ever had any better time in my life than I did digging in the sand, I have failed to recognize it."[11]

When Elder L. Tom Perry was growing up, his family set aside every Saturday afternoon as family playtime. During the summers, the family would

7 Eleanor Knowles, *Howard W. Hunter* (1994), 26–27.
8 Mary Jane Woodger, *David O. McKay: Beloved Prophet* (2004), 94.
9 Bruce C. Hafen, *A Disciple's Life: The Biography of Neal A. Maxwell* (2002), 224.
10 *Life Lessons from Fathers of Faith,* comp. Gary W. Toyn and Michael K. Winder (2010), 60–61.
11 *Teachings of Presidents of the Church: John Taylor* (2001), 191.

go up the canyon to fish, hike, play ball, and picnic together. In the winter, they would play card or board games together.[12]

President Russell M. Nelson took special steps to ensure he had adequate playtime with his son after his call to the apostleship. After returning from long trips, he would occasionally check his son out of school for half a day to go skiing together. "[President] Nelson has long concurred with the counsel of President Harold B. Lee: 'The most important of the Lord's work you will ever do will be within the walls of your own homes'—or on the ski slopes with your children and grandchildren."[13]

Some families enjoy cooking and baking together—bread, cookies, doughnuts, or whatever draws family members in. When President Joseph Fielding Smith was a young father, he would occasionally delve into the art of pie-baking. Donning an apron and sending kids scurrying for ingredients, everyone enjoyed smelling the pies and cranking the ice-cream freezer in anticipation.[14]

Many families prioritize playtime together with a weekend evening set aside for a movie or game night. These evenings can become a wonderful tradition to build happy memories and strong relationships. Decide in family council which movie you will watch and what treats you will share. Some families make food official with pizza or popcorn or cookies each week. You can rotate each week who chooses the movie or treat, or everyone can vote and agree on one together. (Often, solidifying your choice will require some family members to compromise. You can reassure them that learning to compromise is an excellent life skill and perhaps their vote can have more sway the next week.)

Other families prefer to hold weekly family game nights. These can also be planned and agreed on in family council. Pull out a board or card game or choose another activity. Appendix II lists some ideas to get you thinking.

When our oldest child started kindergarten, I realized that the pull of social interaction with friends would become increasingly stronger as he got older, and I wanted our family to still provide a home base of fun, love, and laughter. We decided to institute family fun night. Family fun night has evolved through the years, but the basis is a fun meal followed by a family activity in a weekend time slot. For years, when my children were younger, family fun night every week was homemade mac and cheese followed by an outing or activity. Now we choose the dinner and the activity each week in family council. In the summer we lean toward outdoor activities—campfires, swimming, parks, hiking, or campouts. In the winter we choose more movie and game nights. The important thing is that our family regularly enjoys time playing and being together.

12 *L. Tom Perry: An Uncommon Life, Years of Preparation* (2013), 60–61.
13 Spencer J. Condie, *Russell M. Nelson: Father, Surgeon, Apostle* (2003), 84.
14 *Teachings of Presidents of the Church: Joseph Fielding Smith* (2013), 74.

I also like to start the summer by brainstorming outing ideas with my kids. Together we drum up a list of parks, hikes, or other inexpensive activities everyone would enjoy. We often pack a picnic or some snacks and go enjoy just being together. In the summer when my kids gravitate toward extra time with their friends, I love setting aside time we spend together playing and building memories.

Families today are busy, and diligently scheduling time for your family to play together and enjoy the sweetness of your family unit allows relationships to grow stronger.

Building Family Traditions

When game nights, movie nights, or other forms of play are consistently woven into the fabric of family life, they begin to form family traditions. Wise parents carefully consider family traditions that will create bonds and facilitate wholesome recreation time. Weekly game nights, family home evening, and consistent habits of Sabbath observance are all examples of family traditions that lend flavor and stability to a family unit.

Often the term *family traditions* brings to mind visions of annual holiday events: Independence Day parades or fireworks, Thanksgiving dinners, Easter basket exchanges, or live Christmas nativities. These kinds of traditions are important in drawing families together in happy rituals. Consider your family's traditions and whether they are meeting the desired needs.

Many years ago, Elder L. Tom Perry started a tradition of gathering his family at Bear Lake. His son shared, "When we started going to Bear Lake . . . it was not my father's intention to continue the tradition for more than twenty years. . . . In the beginning, he would ask us each year if we should go to Bear Lake the next year or try out another place." Over time as family members continued to choose Bear Lake, all the family's memories centered on that particular destination, and everyone anticipated the annual trip. Elder Perry believed "in assessing whether a new family tradition [fulfilled] its intended purpose . . . Like any successful long-term investor, . . . he [diversified] risk by establishing and maintaining a wide variety of family traditions. He [knew] some traditions [would] have more staying power than others, but all of them [were] investments in an eternal family."[15]

Sometimes traditions start almost unwittingly, but everyone enjoys them and they fall into the routine of family life effortlessly. If this occurs, roll with it and embrace the security and familiarity everyone feels from a happy, predictable routine. Other times, as families age and expand, some traditions

15 *L. Tom Perry: An Uncommon Life, Years of Preparation* (2013), 166–67.

need to be retired. If a tradition no longer serves its purpose of unifying family members, treasure the memories and let it go.

Purposeful Traditions

Proactive parents consider what messages they want their family traditions to teach. Many traditions serve a simple but important purpose of creating family time and happy memories. But some holidays offer excellent opportunities for traditions that instill specific values.

In the beginning of our marriage, Cameron and I sat down to think of family traditions that would teach our children significant concepts. Feeling young and ambitious, the list we compiled was quite comprehensive. Some of these traditions are events we look forward to every year. Others are ideas we have only used once or twice. Some are ideas we have observed from the examples of others. If you are looking for some meaningful ideas for family traditions, here are a few we have enjoyed in our home or that we have seen other families use:

VALENTINE'S DAY

Although it is traditionally thought of as a romantic holiday, Valentine's Day is a wonderful time to celebrate love between family members. Years ago we took a cue from a mother who would assign her children as secret pals to each other for the week leading up to Valentine's Day. We call it Cupid Week, and we kick it off by opening a little "store" in our room where the kids can come in and choose a couple of simple, inexpensive treats we've purchased that they can surprise their secret pal with during the week. We encourage them to supplement these surprises with other small acts of service such as writing a loving note or making a sibling's bed. Many years we have chosen a family night to cut out hearts and heart attack neighbors. Some moms I know put a heart on each child's door every day for the week or two leading up to Valentine's Day. Each heart has a specific compliment or thing they love about that child. We like to finish Valentine's Day with a nice dinner and a heartfelt note for each of our children expressing some of the things we love and admire about them.

ST. PATRICK'S DAY

Cameron and I like to tell our family that a service brownie elf (or a leprechaun) is visiting our home. We make a large paper shamrock to initiate the service chain. One of us will do an act of service for a family member and leave the shamrock out where the service was performed. When that family member finds the shamrock, she can then do an act of service for another family member and leave the shamrock for him to find.

APRIL 6

This is a wonderful day to celebrate Christ's birth and the organization of the Church. You can go all-out with a birthday cake or by eating foods Jesus might have eaten such as fish, cantaloupe, honey, or dates and figs. For a simpler observance you can read parts of Doctrine & Covenants 20 or 21. Video segments depicting the organization of the Church are available on lds.org.

EASTER

We love to build up to the joy of Easter morning by celebrating the Holy Week leading up to Sunday morning. We start on Palm Sunday with a reenactment of Christ's triumphal entry. Cameron is typically the donkey, and other family members wave palm branches (in the form of green towels) and shout Hosanna as we imagine watching the Savior's entry. On Monday we discuss Christ cleansing the temple. On Tuesday we focus on parables Christ taught the last week of His life (see Matthew 25 for a few ideas). On Wednesday we discuss more parables or talk about Judas's tragic choice to betray Christ. On Thursday we celebrate the Passover as a family with a Passover meal and a discussion about the Last Supper. On Friday we discuss the Crucifixion.[16] On Saturday we talk about Christ in the spirit world sending missionaries out to teach the spirits in spirit prison (see D&C 138). We might celebrate with regional foods from our missions and talk about the missions our children will one day serve. On Easter Sunday we like to eat popovers for breakfast. These light rolls are hollow like Christ's tomb, and we like to fill them with yogurt and whipped cream while we bear our testimonies of Christ's Resurrection. We also like to eat fish and honeycomb for Easter dinner as Christ did in Luke 24:42. We choose an earlier day for Easter baskets, candy, and Easter egg hunts so Sunday morning can be left solely for the joy of Christ's victory. We supplement our celebration on many of these days with gospel artwork, *The Life of Jesus Christ Bible Videos,* and accounts from the scriptures of Christ's life and Atonement.

Another family we know sets out a basket of service Easter eggs. In the week or two leading up to Easter, family members can write down each act of service they perform and put it in an Easter egg. All the eggs are read during

---

16 For young children, we love to read the book *In the Garden* by Caralyn Buehner. It explains Christ's sacrifice in simple, beautiful terms.

Easter dinner, and the family celebrates the goodness they have spread as they remember the Savior's sacrifice.[17]

RESTORATION OF THE PRIESTHOOD

Choose a family night in May to recognize the Restoration of the priesthood. If you would like, you can go to a river and talk about Joseph and Oliver's experience when Peter, James, and John appeared to restore the Melchizedek Priesthood on the banks of the Susquehanna River. Youth can be encouraged to memorize Doctrine & Covenants 13. It's only one verse, but it contains the words John the Baptist said when he conferred the priesthood upon Joseph Smith and Oliver Cowdery.

MEMORIAL DAY

We like to tell stories about ancestors, look at pictures, and visit gravesides when possible. You can use this holiday to help your children feel connected to ancestors who have sacrificed in the past. Eat traditional family foods or recipes, play games, and sing songs that are meaningful to your family. We enjoy taking our children to decorate or clean family gravestones. On some of these cemetery excursions we have seen other large family groups gathered at their ancestors' graves. Sometimes they are sitting on lawn chairs laughing, visiting, and enjoying each other. One time we saw a family who had brought a card table laden with food for all the relatives to share. I couldn't help admiring the way they gathered their family to share and remember.

INDEPENDENCE DAY

We love to teach our children that America was founded under the Lord's guidance and blessing. We enjoy a Fourth of July breakfast (red, white, and blue pancakes or waffles topped with strawberries, blueberries, and whipped cream). Sometimes we read the Declaration of Independence together and discuss the importance of freedom.[18] Help your children understand that the gospel had to be restored in a land where religious freedom was present, so our Father in Heaven was intimately involved in the founding of America.

17 For other specific ideas on celebrating Holy Week as a family, I recommend *A Christ-Centered Easter* by Janet Hales or *The Holy Week for Latter-day Saint Families* by Wendee Wilcox Rosborough.

18 If your children are younger, a variety of children's books explain important stories from our nation's beginnings. We love *When Washington Crossed the Delaware* and *We the People: The Story of Our Constitution* by Lynne Cheney, as well as the picture-book version of *Seven Miracles That Saved America* by Chris and Ted Stewart.

BACK TO SCHOOL

Celebrate the beginning of new knowledge and wisdom with either a special family dinner on the first day of school or a special family outing the weekend before. Teach your children that knowledge is godly and they will take what they learn into the eternities.

SEPTEMBER 21

Recognize the day Joseph Smith received the gold plates from the angel Moroni and testify of the Book of Mormon. A couple of times we have acted this momentous event out as a family. Let children take turns being Joseph and carrying a pillowcase with a heavy book or rock inside. Other children can take turns being the mobbers who tried to get the plates from Joseph. The family member playing the part of Joseph might find some creative strategies to escape. You could also make gold plates out of Rice Krispies treats by giving everyone a rectangle and letting them add some frosting hieroglyphics.

THANKSGIVING

We took a cue from Joshua 4, in which the priests were commanded to gather twelve stones to keep as a memorial of the Lord parting the Jordan River for them. The stones were to remind future generations of how the Lord had led and blessed the children of Israel. For a week or two leading up to Thanksgiving we pass around a little bowl of twelve decorative stones each night at dinner. Each person removes a stone and says something the Lord blessed them with that day. We keep passing until all the stones are taken.

DECEMBER 23

Celebrate Joseph Smith's birthday by reading sections of the First Vision together and bearing testimony of Joseph Smith's divine mission. Alternatively, you can read Doctrine & Covenants 76:22–24, and talk about how Joseph Smith was a witness of Christ.

CHRISTMAS

We like to choose a variety of Christmas activities and traditions that involve Nativity symbols and discuss them throughout the season. We like to drive around and look at Christmas lights and talk about how Christ is the Light of the World, carol and talk about the angel choir which sang at Christ's birth, make and wrap gifts and talk about the Wise Men, and choose a specific service project and talk about how we would give to Jesus if He were here. On

Christmas Eve we have a family devotional and write our annual gifts to Jesus (personal goals we set to follow Christ more closely) and put them in a special stocking we hang in Jesus's honor.[19]

BIRTHDAYS

One family we know helped their child organize a service party for her birthday one year. In lieu of presents the guests brought things that would be donated to a local hospital. Instead of looking at what she would receive, their child learned the joy of giving.

The role of parents in creating consistent traditions to build bonds and strengthen the family unit cannot be overstated. Consider what you want to teach and how you want to achieve memories of wholesome fun together. What do family members enjoy doing together? Counsel with your spouse and talk to your children. Establish traditions that will help create an eternal family unit.

Family Dinner

One critical tradition parents can establish is a happy family dinnertime. Citing studies that family meals are "the strongest predictor of children's academic achievement and psychological adjustment"[20] as well as "a strong bulwark against children's smoking, drinking, or using drugs," President Dallin H. Oaks taught, "There is inspired wisdom in this advice to parents: what your children really want for dinner is you."[21]

Sometimes coordinating schedules is difficult. Children don't always want to prioritize family mealtime. Elder Robert D. Hales shared a time when he was young and wanted to play baseball with his friends instead of coming in for dinner; he asked his mother to save his meal for him in the oven. She responded, "Robert, I really want you to take a break, come home, be with the family for dinner, and then you can go out and play baseball until dark." Elder Hales said, "She taught all of us that where family meals are concerned, it's not the food but the family interaction that nourishes the soul."[22]

---

19 For other Christmas traditions ideas, I recommend *Celebrating a Christ-Centered Christmas* by Emily Belle Freeman.

20 Jared R. Anderson and William J. Doherty, "Democratic Community Initiatives: The Case of Overscheduled Children," *Family Relations*, vol. 54 (Dec. 2005): 655, as cited in Dallin H. Oaks, "Good, Better, Best," *Ensign*, Nov. 2007, 106.

21 Dallin H. Oaks, "Good, Better, Best," *Ensign*, Nov. 2007, 106.

22 Robert D. Hales, "Our Duty to God: The Mission of Parents and Leaders to the Rising Generation," *Ensign*, May 2010, 95–96.

I love the careful way his mother handled that situation. She did not make orders or demands; she kindly requested and explained her reasons. It is easier for a child to comply when parents are respectful, loving, and consistent.

Making family mealtime happen regularly will often require sacrifice, flexibility, and commitment. As activities and seasons come and go in families, different needs must be considered. Many families set a family rule about media usage during dinner—leave phones and other screens alone and focus on each other. Some nights different schedules and activities will make a formal dinner with everyone present impossible. Other times family dinner will require stretching and creativity. At one point in our family, when having dinner together was requiring extra work from me, I started to feel tired and wondered why I was working so hard. Then one day the Spirit spoke to me: "Why do you expect something that's important to come easily?" Family dinner is important. It is worth sacrificing for. It takes commitment. But it is worth it. We only achieve true success when we keep trying. Make a commitment to hold family dinner, and then make it again and again as needs change.

Family dinners provide an important place for families to connect, share the day's events, laugh, coordinate, and enjoy each other. Some nights just gathering everyone together to eat in one place is a major accomplishment. Other nights you might feel more energetic and your family may be ready to add some extra activities into the mix to make things fun. In addition to normal conversation and sharing with each other, some families choose a few favorite dinner games to keep the meal light and enjoyable. Appendix III lists a series of questions to spur conversation at dinner. You can copy them off, cut them up, put them in a jar, and pass the jar around the table when you need a conversation pickup. Add some of your own or omit those that don't suit your purposes. Let someone choose a question, and let everyone answer. Enjoy the opportunity to laugh and get to know each other better. The next night, choose a different question.

In addition to conversation starters, there are a few games that adapt well to a family meal setting. Here are some ideas to consider:

TWENTY QUESTIONS

Our family loves to play a variety of guessing games. These work well because they can involve even the youngest family members. On Sunday we play scripture hero guessing games. Other days we challenge each other to guess a food, an animal, a person, or another item.

JUST A MINUTE

We took this idea from the BBC program by the same name. In this game we set a timer for sixty seconds and assign a family member a topic. The challenge is to give a succinct speech without repeating words or saying "um." We keep a desk bell handy so other family members can ring it and challenge the speaker on repetition, hesitation, or deviation, and one parent acts as the judge to decide whether the charge is accepted. If the challenge was judged valid, the topic is passed on to the challenger for the remaining time. The one who finishes the topic successfully at the end of the sixty seconds wins the round. You can adjust the topic to the age of the recipient or the day of the week. We have had some delightful speeches about scripture heroes and favorite Church songs, along with more ordinary topics such as animals or foods. This gives children confidence to think on their feet, gather their thoughts, and share their ideas in a fun atmosphere.

PICNIC BASKET

This is a classic memory game. The first person says, "I'm going on a picnic, and I'm taking a picnic basket and a water bottle." Each subsequent person repeats the first items and adds an additional item. Items often become humorous and lighthearted, but family members are using their memory while having fun.

ALPHABET GAMES

These can be adapted to a younger or older audience. If your children are young, go around the table and see how many foods or animals you can name that start with the letter *a*, and then move on to the letter *b*, and so on. If your children are older, name countries, cities, important historical figures, family members, or anything else that strikes your fancy.

GROUP STORYTELLING

This activity starts with one person beginning a story. For example, they might say, "One day I was walking down the street and I saw . . ." Then the story passes to another family member. Again, this works best if one parent acts as a mediator and passes the story to the next person at appropriate times. We love this game for the way it gets imaginations going. We have had some wild stories about family members, aliens, monsters, and animals.

In addition to playing games at dinner, some families find that mealtimes easily blend with light educational items. Dinner or breakfast can be great times to recite scriptures or quotes you are trying to memorize as a family. One father I know likes to ask his children each night at dinner what good thing they did for someone that day. When Cameron was growing up, his mother would sometimes keep a map of the world underneath a clear vinyl tablecloth. This provided a wonderful way for the family to explore, discover, and discuss together. They also bought plastic placemats from the different places they had traveled on family vacation. When the vacation placemats were set out, family members could reminisce and talk about their travels. Other families have placemats with math facts, the alphabet, the solar system, or other items for childhood learning. One family I know holds occasional manners nights with fine china and place settings and uses the opportunity to teach and practice etiquette. All of these ideas provide opportunities to learn and discuss in a family environment.

Having fun as a family is essential for family members to form strong bonds and build an eternal family unit. Parents must make conscious efforts to schedule and create fun through daily, weekly, or annual traditions that gather family members in a spirit of love, togetherness, and lighthearted fun.

Application

1. Once or twice a year, counsel with your spouse and children and pray about your family's calendar. Are there commitments you could release to lessen stress and give your family more time together?

2. Consistently watch your calendar and schedule times for your family to play together. Have a movie night, play a board game, or refer to some of the ideas in Appendix II for ideas. Laugh and enjoy each other!

3. Consider wise limits you might place on your screen time. Teach your children the importance of managing their screen time, and set appropriate boundaries for them.

4. Consider your family's traditions. Do they reinforce the values you try to teach? Periodically evaluate traditions to see which ones should be retired or which new ones might be adopted.

5. Make a commitment to have regular family dinners. Make it again and again as your family's schedule and needs change.

6. Consider some games to make family dinners even more enjoyable. (Refer to Appendix III for conversation starters.)

EPILOGUE

Let's strive for steady improvement without obsessing over . . . 'toxic perfectionism.'—Jeffrey R. Holland[1]

IN OUR HOME HANGS A quote I love by President Gordon B. Hinckley: "It isn't as bad as you sometimes think it is. It all works out. Don't worry. I say that to myself every morning. It will all work out. If you do your best, it will all work out. Put your trust in God, and move forward with faith and confidence in the future. The Lord will not forsake us."[2] I have found this to be appropriate counsel for many aspects of life, especially for families. In parenting we must press forward with faith and hope, even when our children's choices don't merit much confidence. We must trust the Lord to be with us and light the way.

As you progress through your parenting journey and work to implement changes, be patient with yourself and your children. Trust that the Lord won't forsake you and everything will work out in His time and in His way. Do the best you can, and don't beat yourself up for mistakes you make. Consider the words of Elder Jeffrey R. Holland, "Every one of us aspires to a more Christlike life than we often succeed in living. If we admit that honestly and are trying to improve, we are not hypocrites; we are human."[3] God knew He was not sending your children to a perfect family. Trust the Savior and His grace to strengthen you and help your family despite your shortcomings.

Consider the miracle of the loaves and fishes in Matthew 14. Despite the fact that the disciples could only offer five small loaves and two fishes, the Savior fed the multitude. Sometimes in parenting our offerings are similarly

---

1 Jeffrey R. Holland, "Be Ye Therefore Perfect—Eventually," *Ensign*, Nov. 2017, 42.
2 Gordon B. Hinckley, "Latter-day Counsel: Excerpts from Addresses of President Gordon B. Hinckley," *Ensign*, Oct. 2000, 73.
3 Holland, "Be Ye Therefore Perfect—Eventually," 42.

meager; trust the Lord to make it enough. As you make small changes to be more forgiving, patient, loving, and compassionate, over time your nature can change. Slowly these Christlike choices become more natural and instinctive. The Atonement of Jesus Christ extends second chances. Pray, repent, apologize, and try again. In that simple process you teach your children doctrines of repentance, forgiveness, and hope offered through Christ.

It is easy to feel down when your children don't respond to your example, testimony, and teachings the way you hope they will. If that is the case, you are not alone. Many similar examples can be drawn from the scriptures, beginning with our premortal existence, when not all of our Heavenly Father's children embraced His plan. While it is easy to get caught in an endless web of why and if-only questions, these thought patterns don't bring healing. Turning your heart and your children over to the Savior is the only way to find peace.

I like President Howard W. Hunter's counsel to parents: "A successful parent is one who has loved, one who has sacrificed, and one who has cared for, taught, and ministered to the needs of a child."[4] Despite the choices of your children, if you are fulfilling your responsibility to love and nurture them, you have truly succeeded with the matters you can control. Don't be too hard on yourself; it won't help you or anyone else. A loving Father in Heaven allows all of us to make choices and learn from the consequences. He does not ask you to make your child perfect—that is the Savior's role. What He does ask is that you love your children and teach them as well as you can.

When I served as the Relief Society president of my ward, I worried about some of the sisters in my stewardship and about their choices and circumstances. One night I was deeply concerned about one particular sister whose decisions had created serious difficulties, and I knelt to pour out my feelings to the Lord. In the eyes of the world this sister could have been judged harshly for a series of long-reaching mistakes. But as I prayed I was overwhelmed with a feeling of love for this sister. I understood that in the Lord's eyes, she wasn't a sinner to condemn; she was His beloved daughter. She was alone and afraid, and He wanted me to love her, show compassion, and care for her. I couldn't fix everything, and that wasn't what He wanted. He was her Parent, and she was in His hands. All He needed was for me to truly love her.

God views each of us with equal deep love and compassion. You and your children are in His care. He knows the experiences you need and the situations that can help you and your family prepare to return to Him. Trust His hand. Counsel with Him. Above all, love your children. Keep your faith and hope

---

4 *Teachings of Presidents of the Church: Howard W. Hunter* (2015), 228.

in your Heavenly Father's plan for your child and the atoning grace of Jesus Christ.

Whatever your circumstances, strive to build a family of faith by the choices you make in your home. Shine the light of your personal discipleship as you love the Lord and live the principles outlined in the family proclamation. In a darkening world, your children need a parent who will strive to live the gospel, teach, and testify. Bonnie L. Oscarson has encouraged, "Let us help build the kingdom of God by standing up boldly and being defenders of marriage, parenthood, and the home. The Lord needs us to be brave, steadfast, and immovable warriors who will defend his plan and teach the upcoming generations His truths."[5] I love the rich imagery of this quote: God needs us to be warriors! Sometimes, getting through the daily demands of family life feels like a battle, doesn't it? But in reality we are engaged in a battle that involves our children and potentially their children and grandchildren. We fight this battle by consciously working to flood our homes with prayer and faith. We protect our children in the world's battles as we fill them with respect, love, and compassion. We fortify our families in the battle as we repent and forgive and work and play together. We are engaged in a battle for the souls of our family members and others around us. Our personal discipleship and parenting choices can do much to fill our homes with light despite the darkness of the world.

May we each heed the battle call and rise to the challenge as we strive to live the principles of the family proclamation in our homes.

---

5 Bonnie L. Oscarson, "Defenders of the Family Proclamation," *Ensign*, May 2015, 17.

APPENDIX I
Interview Questions

- What are you excited about?
- What are you worried about?
- What makes you feel loved?
- What is one thing about our family you wish were different?
- What is your favorite/least favorite thing about our family?
- Who are your closest friends? What do you like to do with them?
- Is there anything about our family that is embarrassing to you?
- Are there any hobbies or interests you would like to explore? How can we help?
- What was the best thing that happened to you last month (week)?
- What are your favorite/least favorite things about school?
- Has anything happened recently that made you uncomfortable?
- Do you have any goals you would like to set? How can we help you?
- When do you feel happiest? Why?
- What is your biggest challenge right now? How can we help?
- Have you noticed anyone who needs our help? What could we do to serve them?
- When you picture your life in two years, what do you picture? What would you like to do?
- Have you felt the Holy Ghost this month? Tell me about that.
- What is your favorite memory from last year?
- What have you read or learned about lately that was interesting?
- What is the best part of your life right now?

APPENDIX II
25 Weeks of Family Fun

1. Play hide-and-seek or sardines (hide-and-seek in which everyone tries to find the hider. When each person finds the hider, they stay there until everyone is crammed into one little spot together).
2. Play crab soccer. Kick a ball around together, but everyone is on all fours, bellies up.
3. Play keep-away. One person in the middle tries to get the ball while everyone else throws it back and forth to each other and tries to avoid the person who is "it."
4. Play What Time Is It, Mr. Fox? Someone is chosen to be Mr. Fox, and everyone else calls out, "What time is it, Mr. Fox?" Mr. Fox responds by saying a time, and everyone takes the number of steps given in the time (if Mr. Fox responds, "Three o'clock," everyone takes three steps). When everyone is close, Mr. Fox responds by saying, "It's dinnertime!" or "It's midnight!" and tries to tag someone to be the next Mr. Fox.
5. Have a water fight with water guns or other water toys.
6. Host an indoor snowball fight with a laundry hamper full of sock balls.
7. Have a flour fight. Fill knee-high nylons with a cup each of flour and tie them off, and then go to your backyard and have a free-for-all. You don't need many flour bombs, because each can be used over and over. And when you're finished you can store them for another time. This makes for messy laundry but great pictures!
8. Set up a miniature golf course in your house or backyard.
9. Have a relay race. Set up a course in your house or yard and split your family into teams. Be zany and creative—this can be a lot of fun.
10. Play sharks and minnows. One person is the shark, and when it's time to start, all the minnows try to run past the shark without being tagged and becoming sharks themselves. Continue until all the minnows have become sharks.

11. Play Marco Polo. One person is blindfolded and calls out "Marco," and everyone responds with "Polo." Marco tries to catch someone to be the next Marco. This works great in the yard, but in the winter can be played inside in a cleared room (be careful, and watch out for potential hazards Marco could run into or trip over).
12. Play charades or picture-guessing games. Make up a fun list of items for people to act out or draw, and split up into teams to guess the subject of the actions or drawings.
13. Bake cookies together (or whatever else your family might enjoy).
14. Have a sing-along of Disney or Broadway music (or whatever other songs you like).
15. Make pudding artwork. Give each person a cup of pudding, a plate, some utensils, and whatever decorations you want, and let each person paint something on their plate.
16. Do basement bowling. Set up a pyramid with cans or even toilet paper rolls and go bowling.
17. Make gingerbread houses out of graham crackers, frosting, and whatever else you have on hand.
18. Play a board game.
19. Take a picnic to a park, or sit on your floor with a picnic blanket and watch a movie.
20. Play dodgeball.
21. Build a blanket fort and read books together.
22. Build pyramids or other structures with marshmallows and toothpicks.
23. Do a puzzle together.
24. Have a homemade play dough sculpture contest. Make a variety of play-dough colors, and let people use their creativity.
25. Play apple truck. A parent is the farmer, and the kids are the apples. The farmer tries to get the apples and load them into the truck (couch). When all the apples have been gathered, the game restarts. But be careful, sometimes the apples escape when the farmer isn't looking! (It's best to choose a set space, such as one room, for this game.)

APPENDIX III
Family Dinner Conversation-Starters

- Name one place you'd like to go on vacation, and tell us why. What would we do there?
- Name one scripture hero. What do you admire about this person?
- Tell us one silly or happy thing from your day.
- Tell us one sad or frustrating thing from your day.
- Tell us about a time when you were embarrassed.
- "I wish it would rain _____." (Fill in the blank—doughnuts, quarters, flowers, gumdrops, etc.) What would you do if it did rain _____?
- What is your favorite holiday and why?
- Tell us one thing you love about one of your grandparents.
- If you were an animal, what would you want to be and why?
- If you had three wishes, what would they be?
- Tell us one thing that really happened and one thing that didn't. We'll guess what's what.
- Share a favorite family memory, vacation, family fun night, etc.
- If you had a hundred dollars, what would you buy?
- Tell us one nice thing you did for someone this week.
- Name someone whom we could serve. What should we do?
- What is usually your favorite part of your day?
- What is your favorite game to play with our family? Why?
- Name a favorite book and tell us why you like it.
- What do you think you would have liked or disliked about being a pioneer?
- What is your favorite family tradition we have?
- Think of a storybook character. Help us guess who it is.
- If you could spend a day with Joseph Smith, what day would you want it to be?

- Name one story from Jesus's life that you wish you could have been there to see.
- Name a favorite movie and tell us why.
- What's your favorite food and why?
- Describe the perfect day—what would you do?
- What is your favorite time of year and why?
- What is your favorite holiday and why?
- Pretend to be an animal. Let us guess what it is.
- Think of a fruit or vegetable. Let us guess what it is.
- Find something in the room. Let us guess what it is.
- If you could have a superpower, what would you choose?
- Name one thing you're really good at.
- Name one thing another family member is really good at.
- What qualities are important in a friend?
- What is your favorite part of our meal tonight and why?
- Ask a family member any question you want.
- Which do you like better: sledding or swimming? Why?
- What was your favorite part of your birthday last year? What do you remember?
- What was your favorite present from last Christmas or your last birthday?
- Name one thing that scares you.
- If you could trade places with a family member for a day, who would you be and why?
- If you could have one dream come true, what would it be?
- What do you want to be doing in ten years?
- Name one place you think would be an interesting place to serve a mission, and tell us why.
- If you could have one pet, what would it be?
- Name one nice thing someone did for you recently.
- What do you want to be when you grow up?
- If you could only eat five things for a month, what would they be?
- What is one thing you wish you knew how to do?
- What would you do if you were a king or queen?
- If you were invisible, where would you go?
- Which would you prefer: a trip to the zoo or a trip to the beach?
- What is your favorite thing to do at the park?
- Tell us a favorite scripture story.

- "If a dragon came to dinner, I would _____." (Fill in the blank.)
- What would you like to invent?
- Name one thing you like to do.
- If you had to move and only take three things, what would you take?
- What would you like to do to make the world better?
- Name three things you're thankful for.
- What makes you laugh?
- What do you do when you can't fall asleep?
- What's your favorite outdoor/indoor activity?
- Would you rather hike to a waterfall or a cave?
- What are three words to describe how you feel right now?
- If you could change your age, how old would you be?
- What three qualities would you like to have?
- What do you think we should do to make our family stronger?
- Think of a member of our extended family. Let us guess who it is.
- What is your favorite job around the house?
- What is your favorite thing to grow in our garden?
- Would you rather spend the night in a tree house or tent?
- Would you rather ride on a train or submarine?
- What kind of dinosaur would you like to be?
- What do you like better: cake or pie?
- Tell us about one day you would like to go back and relive.
- Tell us something you admire about someone.
- If you had a day to do anything you wanted, what would you do?
- If you were one of the three little pigs, what would you have done differently?
- Would you rather be Snow White or Cinderella/Robin Hood or Prince Charming?
- Would you like to be a baby for a day? Why or why not?
- What would you do to tell someone you loved them if you couldn't say it?
- What are five things you would take to a desert island?
- What would you do if you were Goldilocks?
- If you were Mom or Dad for a day, what would you do?
- If you could stay up all night, what would you do?
- What animal do you wish could talk? What questions would you ask them?
- What are the best and hardest things about your life right now?

- I can tell someone loves me when they _____. (Fill in the blank.)
- Which one of the seven dwarfs would you be?
- If you could have a magic wand for a day, what would you do?
- What's a family tradition you would like to start?
- How can we make our family better?
- If snow could fall in any flavor, what would you choose?
- If you're having a bad day, what makes you feel better?
- What do you do that makes people laugh?
- If the prophet were coming for dinner, what would you want to serve?
- If you could ask the prophet one question, what would it be?
- Would you rather have a pet tiger or pet elephant?
- If you could choose any food in the world to put on a pizza, what would it be?
- If you could meet one person from the scriptures, who would it be?

ABOUT THE AUTHOR

RACHEL A. SULLIVAN GREW UP in Anchorage, Alaska, and if she could sit down with you, she would love to tell you tales of her igloo home, pet polar bear, and dog team she mushed to school across the frozen tundra. Unfortunately none of those stories would be true; she lived in a house, had a pet dog, and rode the school bus across icy but paved streets.

Rachel holds a BA in English from BYU with a minor in marriage, family, and human development. She served in the Virginia Richmond Mission, where she fell in love with Southern people, Southern food, and the scriptures. Rachel is passionate about teaching and testifying of the gospel of Jesus Christ to people of all ages.

Rachel is married to her sweetheart, Cameron, and they are the parents of four children. Rachel tries to embrace as much of the joyful messiness of family life as she can; when life becomes too much, she pulls out her karaoke machine for a bit of musical therapy.